IMAGES
of Scotland

AROUND LEV

LUNDIN TOWER, LEVEN

Lundin Tower, early 1900s. The modern part of the old manor house was removed in 1876, leaving this magnificent ivy-clad tower, built before 1500.

IMAGES
of Scotland

AROUND LEVEN

Ena Caldwell

TEMPUS

First published 2000
Copyright © Ena Caldwell, 2000

Tempus Publishing Limited
The Mill, Brimscombe Port,
Stroud, Gloucestershire, GL5 2QG

ISBN 0 7524 2105 0

Typesetting and origination by
Tempus Publishing Limited
Printed in Great Britain by
Midway Clark Printing, Wiltshire

Milk delivery at Silverburn Cottages, c.1905. Picture by J. Patrick.

Contents

Ordnance Survey Map 19

6

Introduction

Although little is known of the early days in Levenmouth, there is evidence that the 'Beaker Makers', from around 2,000 BC, were among the earliest settlers in the area. In 1963, three stone graves (cists) were discovered at Ashgrove, Methilhill, one of which had a bronze dagger and a clay beaker with traces of mead, while in 1821 in Aithernie Den, workmen digging moulding sand for Leven foundry discovered a burial site with twenty stone cists, containing urns and charred wooden beads.

The mysterious Picts who lived around AD 300-843 left a carved symbol stone as their legacy. Known as the 'Scoonie Stone', it was discovered in the 1860s near Scoonie Cemetery and is thought to be early Pictish, and dating to around AD 400, because of the Ogham inscription on the left side. It can be seen in the basement of the National Museum of Scotland, Chambers Street, Edinburgh.

Prior to 1051, Macbeth and his wife, Gruoch, gifted the Kirklands of 'Scouni' to the Culdees or Celtic monks of St Serf's Priory at Loch Leven. In the twelfth century, the Priory and its possessions, including 'Scouni', were handed over to the new Priory of St Andrews, of the Roman faith. The ecclesiastical village of 'Scouni' then consisted of a church, a manse and a few houses to accommodate the men and women who were serfs of the church.

In 1435, a small harbour must have existed at Leven with sufficient number of residents able to carry on some shipping trade, as a boat containing twenty carcasses of salted oxen from the King's larder at Stirling was sent from Blackness Castle in Linlithgowshire to Leven, being the nearest port to Falkland.

Wool had long been exported to Flanders and was returned as manufactured goods, while increasingly linen and other fine products of the Flemish and Brabantine weavers were also imported. A law was passed in 1498 encouraging these weavers to bring their families and apprentices to this area – note Emsdorf village and Picardy in Lundin Links – so that no raw material should be reimported as finished goods. It was said that, early in the sixteenth century, a Brabant vessel was wrecked off the coast and the surviving crew were allowed by the Wemyss family to settle and found the village which is now Buckhaven.

In 1546 Alexander of the Maw, a tenant of the Wemyss family, offered to pay for repairing Scoonie Church, referred to then as the Monastery of Levynnis-mouth.

In 1602 smuggling of contraband goods from the Continent was prevalent, and owners and masters of vessels at ports on both sides of the Forth, including Leven, were prohibited from importing or exporting any goods except coal and salt. In 1614, when Leven was more of an expanding village than a town, it was bought by Sir Alexander Gibson of Durie and became a Burgh of Barony. There was built a 'Tolbuth and Tron with ane Mercat Crosse'; the Tolbooth site has never been established, but the Mercat Cross later stood at the top of Carpenter's Brae, off the High Street. The Tolbooth was the jail; the Tron was where goods being traded were weighed and the Mercat Cross was where important news was announced, such as the arrival in Leven of Charles II on 14 February 1651, following his coronation at Scone, when he reviewed the troops on Leven sands.

Coal mining was developed by the Gibsons on Durie Estate and by David, second Earl of Wemyss at his 'Happy Mine', Denbeath. However, at that time, nine out of ten Scots still lived on farm settlements as tenants, smallholders or farm servants. Water leads from the River Leven had provided power from the late twelfth century, primarily to grind meal and flour, but by 1660, further advancements in driving machinery by water power meant that Methil, Scoonie and Kennoway Parishes had meal mills, corn mills, spinning mills, and coal haughs, operated by 'water-gin'.

By the end of the eighteenth century, the 'improvers' were reshaping landscapes and rural communities, while the towns were experiencing an extraordinary expansion of industry and commerce. Farms were enclosed by hedges, fences and walls, steadings were enlarged and workers' housing was improved. Mansion houses were built, surrounded by parkland and avenues of trees, such as Carriston, Newton Hall, Kingsdale, Kilmux and Montrave, the latter built by Major Alexander Anderson and acquired in 1873 by Allan Gilmour, a leading Glasgow ship owner.

In 1785 when Messrs Neilson, Greenhill and Co. leased the Kirkland site, factory weaving and spinning received a boost. Later, under Messrs H. & T. Peter, around 800 workers were engaged in flax dressing, spinning and bleaching in a specially-built gas-lit factory, the first in Scotland, and lived in a newly-built village nearby, complete with school. In Leven, the population increased substantially and locals and incomers found employment in the breweries, five spinning mills, farina works, flour mill, foundry, ropespinning works, sawmill, ochre mill and the brick and tile works.

Changes in the industrial pattern weakened the old church discipline. Previously a kirk session had insisted on a testimonial when a family moved into a parish, but the dissent within the Presbyterian churches which took place from the 1730s meant that membership of a congregation and residence within a parish were not synonymous. Fife was one of the areas where dissenting churches grew most rapidly.

Around 1821 a small quay replaced the natural harbour at Leven but was insufficient for the increasing trade, while the shifting sands at the river mouth still posed a problem. In 1835, imports to Leven Harbour included wheat, barley, malt, coal, flax, stones, slates and timber, while exports included bricks and tiles, ochre, linen cloth, cast iron, oats, potatoes, whisky and yarn.

Coal mining in Levenmouth expanded in 1864 when Messrs Bowman and Company leased the abandoned mine at Denbeath, then the Fife Coal Company, which became the largest mining company in Scotland, moved into the area. J.B. Fernie had earlier sunk a shaft on Kilmux Estate, employing villagers from Baintown and Whalley Den.

The route to the north was partly the Pilgrim's Way from Pettycur via the Standing Stone Road to Cameron Ford – later a wooden bridge – to Kennoway, Baintown, Whalley Den, by West Montrave, and on to St Andrews. Roads were mere tracks, 'formed by the occasional tread of horses, wheels of carts or the footsteps of travellers'. Improvements in vehicular traffic required more substantial roads, but main roads only became suitable for wheeled traffic when the local Turnpike Acts were passed. The coming of the railway had a dramatic impact, however, and was responsible for the growing importance of the coastal towns as summer resorts. The six mile stretch to Leven, completed in 1854, was carried out by Thomas Bouche, the engineer of the ill-fated Tay Bridge.

Leven in 1800 consisted of three or four narrow unmade streets; High Street, Back Street, a few houses by the Shore and Mitchell Street. The Links district was a sandy waste while Commercial Road was a field with the hall bordering it, and all around was cultivated glebe land. Murray Place (now part of Commercial Road) was built in the early 1820s for weavers, and the Links houses began to spring up about thirty years later. During the last thirty years of the nineteenth century, many houses were built, the town flourished and evidence of its prosperity was reflected in the new buildings.

As for commerce, in 1839, Dr Robert Chalmers who golfed on Dubbieside Links said, 'the shops of Leven are more elegant and respectable in appearance than those of any other town of similar size in Fife and perhaps in Scotland'.

One
Locations

Before the First World War, the area north of the Leven railway line was almost entirely rural.
After 1919 an extensive house-building programme was carried out by the Town Council and
the town grew significantly.

Dyke Neuk, c.1900. Many families lived in hamlets around Leven such as Dyke Neuk, Letham,
Scoonie Cotton, Lower Scoonie, Scoonie Burn, Cotton of Durie, Banbeath, Mountfleurie and
Silverhole or Sillerhole. Near Coldstream was another hamlet, Cuffabout, where John
Turnbull, the blacksmith, lived. The rivalry among the farms was expressed in this local rhyme:

Cauldstream and Cuffabout
And Claw the Wa'
Bankhead O'Aithernie
Stands abune them a'.

Cock-Ma-Lane, *c*.1910. This early eighteenth-century cottage would originally have had a thatched roof. Although it is now on the edge of a built-up area, it is still recognizable and was until recently a listed building. This idyllic scene was captured on a picture postcard which was posted a few weeks before the outbreak of the First World War.

Greengates, *c*.1910. The gates have gone but the area is still popular for walking and the road beyond the gates now leads to Glenview Caravan Park and provides access to Letham Glen from the north of the town. Local streets have been given the old names of Dyke Neuk and Greengates.

Sillerhole, 1907. Coal had been mined locally since the late 1600s. Water from Banbeath and Durie Lochs had been used to drive pit engines until engineers drove a mine through the 'tail of the craig' of the Maiden Castle at Kennoway Burns, cutting a water channel from there to Durie Broom, near Sillerhole, so that an abundant supply of water was on tap from the Kennoway Burn. Operations were suspended long before 1907, however, due to continual flooding.

SCOONIE DEN, NEAR LEVEN

Scoonie Den, c.1911. In the days when Scoonie Burn was a roaring river, a den of considerable depth was scooped out. As well as coal being mined locally, ochre was also extracted by the Messrs Landale at their Siller Hole pit and, further up the den, Mr John Anderson operated on the same seam. The outsides of many of the little old houses in Fife were painted annually with an orange or a canary tint and ochre was an important pigment for that process.

11

Scoonie Drive, *c.*1925. In answer to Lloyd George's plea that homes be built fit for returning war heroes, work began in 1920 to build one hundred houses on a site to the east of Scoonie High Road. The estate had single and two-storey cottages and was the only major Fife estate not to include flats. The bowling green, providing an open feature, had a clubhouse designed by Andrew Haxton. The opening ceremony was on 26 May 1921, and rents per annum ranged from £22 for a three-apartment cottage to £29 for a five-apartment cottage.

Deas' Bakehouse at Scoonie bridge, 1964. After closure of the railway line in 1969, the area was landscaped to create a popular walk to the golf courses and to Silverburn Estate. In the nineteenth century at Scoonie bridge, White & Son did a considerable business in the ochre trade, one of the oldest industries in Leven, while in the same period many of the Leven houses were built from bricks manufactured at their Brick and Tile Works.

Links Place, *c*.1909. These houses were built in 1876 by George Wilkie, builder, who lived in nearby Bayview Terrace. Among the first residents were Edgar L. Boase of the Spinning Mill at No.1, and Charles Carlow, Chairman of Fife Coal Company at No.2, while William Grosset, papermaker at Millfield, lived with his family at No.5, prior to their moving to Glenlyon House. David Duncan, dentist, later lived at No.5.

The Berea, 1905. This corner house became a YMCA holiday home. A few years later, Professor S.D. Mazure, 'the most famous eye-testing specialist', used to stay nearby at his summer residence, Sandicroft, 'behind the Coastguard Station' and advertised free eye tests while he was there!

Gladstone Street, 1907. John M. Smith was the grocer and wine merchant in the shop on the corner of Gladstone Street and Waggon Road. After the Second World War the business was owned by Robert A. Seath, and in 1976 Thomas Anderson & Son, butchers, who still trade there, transferred their business from 60 High Street.

Waggon Road, 1903. Horse-drawn bogies transported coal along a wooden-rail waggonway here, from Sauchenbush and Sillerhole pits to Leven harbour, for export to Holland, Norway and the Baltic. The creaking of wheels and rattle of tail chains could be heard day and night. When the pits closed, 'Waggon Road was a fine walk with neat cottages on either side, and on the slopes of the North British Railway, brambles and rose bushes grew in profusion'.

Durie Street, *c*.1905. The two-storeyed house and weavers' houses next to Scoonie Kirk eventually made way for the Co-operative Buildings. At the point where Durie Street forks into the High Street and North Street, a small early eighteenth-century building, 'with its red tiles, white-washed front and boles of windows', was demolished to make way for Malcolm's Stationery Salon in 1909.

Durie Street, *c* 1913. The building on the left was the National Bank of Scotland, which was demolished to make way for the present Clydesdale Bank and shopping development in 1968. James Honeyman Smith, who died in 1940, aged ninety-five, was the bank agent and solicitor there for many years. His son, Frederick J. Smith, was also involved in the family business, which became 'Smith and Grant'.

Durie Street, 1907. The tram, outside the saddlers, was approaching the old Leven Post Office. Next were J. Watt, bootmaker, then A. Thomson & Sons, tailors. The ladies are looking at the 'dainty cakes and pastries' of baker John Ovenstone, who originally came from Pittenweem, and was proprietor of the Durie Tea Rooms. P. Lawson & Son, grocers, were on the corner of Durie Street and Mitchell Street.

Durie Street, c.1910. The garage belonged to the Leven Reform Co-operative Society. Next to St John's Church and Osborne House, right, was the Commercial Bank House, now the Royal Bank, where David Nicoll was solicitor and bank agent. James Methven, Rosebank, Denhead, Kennoway, owned the saddler's shop, right. Many people will remember the white horse – the popular sign of the saddler – which stood in the corner window for over fifty years. Every morning the older men of the town would treat his shop as a 'howff', sitting around the stove exchanging news.

High Street, c.1904. This postcard was sent by a reluctant summer visitor, staying at Mrs Campbell's, Hawthorn Street. Written to his son in Connel Ferry, Argyll, he says, 'I have been here since Saturday. Miserable weather, except Tuesday. Is the hay all in? Are the sheep all dipped? How are you all getting on? You might drop me a note letting me know if you are still milking the cows. Father.'

High Street, c.1906. This shows horse-drawn delivery vehicles outside the early Reform Co-operative Society building in the High Street, while on the opposite side is the shop of Arthur Husband, Family Chemist, at 65 High Street, which he had opened four years earlier. Horses at that time had to become accustomed to passing trams.

High Street, *c* 1930. A contemporary report said that in Leven, 'with commendable enterprise the business men of the burgh have taken care that the shops have kept pace with the needs of the community and the visitors' invasion'. Left, before Cormie's domed building, were Buchanan, chemist, D. Mitchell, jeweller and watchmaker, and John Aitken, grocer. John Aitken, who died in 1947, was a Leven Provost and lived for a time after his retirement in Hawkslaw House, now Hawkslaw Hotel.

High Street, 1940s. T.G. Senior, general draper, owned the shop on the corner of Forth Street and High Street, which had been built by his uncle, David Bain, in around 1867. Mr Senior died in 1947, aged ninety-nine. Next to the Co-operative on the left was William Small, newsagent, then the baker, James A. Lightbody.

High Street, *c.*1906. Adam Spiers owned the corner grocer's shop next to bootmakers Thomas Wilkie & Son, with the striped canopy. Miss Simpson, whose Fancy Warehouse was at No.43, rented upper rooms to Dr Robertson, a visiting surgeon-dentist, who consulted in Leven every Friday for many years. The tramcar is passing David Ballingall's ironmonger's shop.

High Street, *c.*1906. Thomas Porter, a printer and bookseller from Cupar, owned the historic building housing the 'Coast Chronicle Office', left, until his death in February 1902, aged eighty. Arthur Gourlay was the stationer in 1906, renting the premises from Porter's daughter, Isabella. The Misses Johnstone were the last owners of this historic building dating from 1681 and, following their retirement in 1959, it was demolished. The building with the turret was the Royal Bank House where solicitor and bank agent, William Shepherd and his brother, J. Ogilvy Shepherd, practised.

High Street, 1962. The buildings of Alex Munro, Boots and A. Cook were redeveloped a few years later. The premises of Lovat, tailor, on the corner were incorporated into Wilkie's Shoe Shop next door. During and immediately after the Second World War, the Telephone Exchange was housed above Cummings at No.33.

High Street, 1962. Robertson, the baker's business, left, was established by David K. Robertson from Abbotshall, Kirkcaldy, and was continued by his son William. After the Steamboat Inn were housefurnishers, Hardy and Co., while on the corner of High Street and Bank Street was Cumming's Men Shop, built on the site after the 1681 building was demolished in around 1959.

Shorehead, *c.*1916. On the left is 'The Turret', built by Dr John Balfour, uncle of Robert Louis Stevenson. Dr Balfour had originally come to Leven in the late autumn of 1866 to help during an epidemic of cholera, of which the local doctor had just died, and there was a state of panic in the town. After the crisis, he stayed on in Leven at the request of the inhabitants, often being visited by his famous nephew. Also on the left, at 4 High Street, was the old ironmonger's business of John Meikle & Son, established in 1812.

J. Meikle & Son, 4 High Street, *c.*1930. The shops of John Meikle & Son at 4 High Street and 2 Union Street were acquired in 1944 by David Blyth Williamson, who linked the shops by means of a shopping arcade. D.B. Williamson died in 1975 and the business was continued by his wife and daughter until 1981.

Fishing Tackle, Cartridges, Cutlery, Garden Requisites.

Trunks, Bags, &c., Mangles, Brushes, Miners' and Joiners' Tools.

SHIPPING AGENCY for all the Principal Lines.

J. Meikle & Son

Ironmongers

Established 1812 :: LEVEN

Shorehead, *c.*1904. At one time all houses here would have had their gable ends facing the harbour. William Ballingall sold beds and drapery items at Albion House. Around 1860, Michael Wallace had established Wallace & Son, drapers, at 1 Shorehead, selling, among other items, ladies' costumes, maid's jackets and sailors' hats! Forbes T. Wallace, born in 1874, the solicitor and joint bank agent at the British Linen Bank, Forth Street, was Michael's youngest son. C. Hutton and Sons owned the butcher's shop.

Shorehead, *c.*1906. Note the steps leading from the Shorehead to the harbour area. Branch Street is on the left and the building with the flat roof was the 'Economic Drapery Store'. Adjacent to that was Seaview Cottage, where William Ballingall, draper, and his wife, Jessie, lived while Seaview House was the home of Dr Robert Balfour Graham.

Bawbee Bridge, *c*.1902. The River Leven, at Leven, could only be crossed by a ford or by Davie Finlay's coble until 1821, when a suspension bridge for foot passengers was constructed near Leven Mills. It was replaced in 1840 by this bridge, the first to carry traffic. The toll, a halfpenny (bawbee), was also paid by foot passengers, a hardship for people who had to cross it to their work place. Tolls were abolished in 1870, but the present bridge, built in 1957, is still called 'the Bawbee Bridge'.

Swiss Cottage, *c*.1903. This cottage was built beside Leven Mills on the River Leven before 1891. John Kerr, a labourer at the oil mills, lived there at that time with his wife, Susan, and six children. Houses built to resemble Swiss cottages must have been fashionable then – two semi-detached houses, of a different style but similarly named, were built in Waggon Road.

Sawmill Cottages, Leven Mills, *c*.1907. As Leven became more industrialized, many workers lived near their employment, beside the foundry (Leven Vale), Hawkslaw Works (Riverside) and the Leven Mills, where oil mill workers and bone mill workers lived in Mayfield, Swiss and Sawmill Cottages.

Riverside Cottage, *c*.1910. Cottages in Riverside were owned by Henry Balfour & Company and rented to their employees. The Boase Spinning Company also rented some cottages there to their workers. Riverside Cottage was the home of Mr More, who served his apprenticeship in the moulder's shop of Durie Foundry, where he later became foreman.

Leven Vale, 1984. The most distant two-storey houses, right, were in Mayfield Terrace. The entrance to Bleachfield Row, which had originally faced the bleachfield and housed its workers, was directly opposite the low cottages. A Mission Hall, built in 1911 and still in use in the late 1940s, was on the corner of Bleachfield Row and Leven Vale. John Adam, draper, 23 High Street, was a long-time representative of the Mission Committee.

Leven Vale, c.1907. Throughout the nineteenth and early twentieth century, since most employment in the town was to be found in Leven Vale and Riverside, many families lived in that area, as did the works' owners: Henry Balfour at Levenbank, James Anderson Snr at Riverbank House and John Balfour at Elm Park, Leven Mills. The last remaining houses in Leven Vale were demolished in the 1980s.

By the River Leven, March 2000. Recently the riverside area was restored, creating a woodland environment for people to enjoy. The work was undertaken by the Millennium Forest for Scotland Trust and is being maintained by members of the Robert Gough Centre. A platform was constructed to allow disabled fishermen to gain access to the River Leven.

Largo Bay, c.1919. When known as Levynnis Mouth, Leven was only a small fishing hamlet, but later fishing in the River Leven and Largo Bay grew in importance and the fishing community flourished. In 1919, H. White of Durie Street advertised 'Fresh haddocks from Largo Bay daily', while Joseph Johnstone & Sons from Montrose leased the salmon fishing from Durie Estate. The salmon bothy, on the left of the picture, was built around 1880 and has recently been demolished. The old coastguard station was possibly the middle building, which was used for storing nets after the new station was built on the Promenade in 1904.

26

Two
Townspeople and Buildings

Leven is indebted to early local photographers, John Patrick, David Gordon, Adam Diston and Ada Smith (nee Mayor) for recording the old town and its people.

R.L. Stevenson and his mother, *c.*1854. John Patrick, born in Buckhaven in 1832, was to become the earliest photographer in Leven at the beginning of the glass plate age. He established a photographic studio at 71 High Street, Leven, where he would have taken this picture of three year old Robert Louis Stevenson and his mother, Margaret, who were frequent visitors to Leven. Patrick later transferred his studio to his home, Photo Villa, Links, Leven. He subsequently opened a studio at 194 High Street, Kirkcaldy, moving to 9 Wemyssfield in 1869, around which time he photographed the elderly Thomas Carlyle on the steps of Provost Swan's house, St Brycedale's. His interest in Scottish writers and places associated with them took him to Edinburgh, where he opened a studio at 52 Comiston Road, later taking his son, James, into partnership with him. Patrick and his sons, James and John Rutherford, were talented painters as well as photographers and exhibited at the Royal Scottish Academy. The Patricks built up an archive of photographs and information on R.L. Stevenson, who had been a friend and correspondent of John R. Patrick until the author's death. John Patrick died at the house of his daughter, Jessie Patrick Findlay, the well-known author, in Den Wynd, Kennoway on 19 May 1923, aged ninety-three. *(Picture courtesy of the Writers' Museum, Lady Stair's House, Lawnmarket, Edinburgh.)*

George Harvey, 1973. In the second half of the twentieth century, many special occasions in the lives of Levenmouth people were captured by the camera of George Harvey. After being demobbed from the Polish Army in 1948, he rented the Promenade Studio, which had belonged to Ada Smith, and built up a very successful business over forty-eight years.

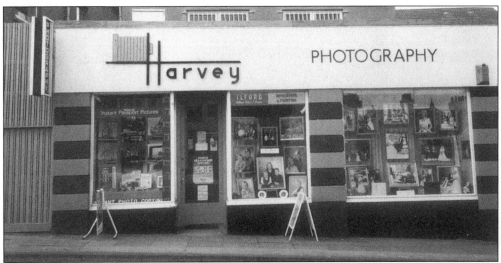

Harvey Studio, 1996. In the 1950s Mr Harvey acquired premises in Commercial Road, Leven, and later opened a shop and studio in Whytecauseway, Kirkcaldy. The Leven premises, above, were extended to accommodate a large, modern studio and processing laboratory. He specialized in portrait, wedding, press and commercial photography. A limited company, formed under Mr Harvey's chairmanship, was dissolved on his retirement in 1996.

Talbot Studio, 1960s. Adam Diston, another of Leven's early 'photographer artists', married Lucy Ann Swinton and they had three sons, James, Alexander and Adam, the latter born in Cupar in 1867 where his father had opened a Bonnygate studio. Diston named his studio in New Station Road, Leven, after pioneer photographer William Fox Talbot (1800-1877), and was succeeded in business in 1889 by his son, Adam, until his sudden death in 1896, aged twenty-eight.

Old White Memorial Hospital, 2000. In 1899 the old Leven Hospital had a new extension generously provided by Provost John White, Mr Thomas White, SSC, and Miss J. White in memory of their mother, Euphemia, and father, Alexander, who had owned the Brick & Tile Works at Scoonie bridge. This isolation hospital, which would take victims of diphtheria epidemics, then common among children, was on the opposite side of the railway line from most of the town.

Jean Donaldson, 1895. In April 1895, Jean Scott Cochrane, daughter of a master draper in Stirling, married George Donaldson, son of the founder of James Donaldson & Sons, Timber Merchants of Tayport and Leven. George was a partner in the firm, responsible for the operation at Wemyss Sawmills, Leven.

Links Road, c.1910. Jean and George Donaldson made their home at 'The Elms', Links Road, Leven. They had two sons, Victor, born in 1898, and Reginald, born in 1902, who would both later be employed in the family business. Reginald looked after the Tayport business while Victor was responsible for the Wemyss Sawmills in Leven.

Reginald and Victor, Stirling 1903. During the First World War, Victor, severely wounded in France while serving with the Black Watch, was sent to Yorkhill Hospital, Glasgow, where he met his future wife, Jean, sister of a fellow patient. Jean was a granddaughter of James Robertson, 'Jammy Jimmy', founder of the 'Golden Shred' Empire of Robertson's Jams. Married in Paisley Abbey on 2 April 1925, they lived outside Lundin Links, at Stanely, a wedding gift from Jean's father, John Robertson.

Jean, George and Reginald at the Elms, c.1923. George Donaldson's Daimler, SP3, which had his monogram painted on the outside, was only the third car in Fife, and was for years driven by his trusty chauffeur, William Thomson. George died in 1937 aged seventy-seven, while Jean lived to be ninety-four and died in 1961.

Charles Carlow, *c*.1905. Shortly after the formation of the Fife Coal Company in Edinburgh in September 1872, officials invited a young mining engineer, Charles Carlow, from the Carberry collieries in the Lothians, to become principal manager of the company. Carlow came to live in Leven, to where the Company's Head Office had been transferred, and which was near his birthplace of Methilhill. He made long journeys on horseback and his white mount became a familiar site on the roads and tracks linking the Company's pits. He eventually became Chairman of the Coal Company and was also Managing Director until his death in 1923.

Linnwood Hall, 1930s. The Carlow family home on the outskirts of Leven, built in 1898.

Levenbank, *c*.1950s. This was the home of Henry Balfour who together with James Anderson, established Durie Foundry. Henry, born in 1797 in Dundee, was the son of Alexander, a well-known Dundee merchant who was Provost there in 1826, 1827 and 1830. In 1818, Henry was a burgess in Dundee. Henry married Agnes Bisset, of Millfield, in 1823, and had sons, Alexander, born 1824, Robert, born 1826, and Henry Thomas, born 1828. Robert and Henry Thomas took over the foundry management from their father, who died at Levenbank on 6 July 1854, aged fifty-seven.

Seaview House, Branch Street, 1985. This was the home of Dr Robert Balfour Graham, Medical Officer of Health for Leven, and his wife, Isabella (Ella) Balfour, only daughter of Henry Thomas Balfour. They later moved to the Balfour family home, Levenbank, then to Barnet, North Links. Their son and grandson were both killed in action in Italy, serving their country in two world wars: Lt R. Balfour Graham with the Black Watch in 1917 and Lt Henry Balfour Graham with the Argyll & Sutherland Highlanders in 1944. Seaview, the 'Doctor's House', was occupied by Dr Malcolm MacNicol around the period of the First World War and, in the 1930s, by Dr J.M. Johnstone.

Norton House, 1986. This was the home of James Anderson Jnr, partner in Henry Balfour & Co., and his wife, Amelia. In the early years of the twentieth century it was owned by Robert Ballingall, before becoming the Earl Haig House in 1931, when it was used by the Leven Branch of the British Legion. Red poppies were incorporated in the wrought iron work around the gate. A few years ago it was demolished, following a fire.

James Anderson of Norton House, 1890s. Mr Anderson worked with Robert and Henry Thomas Balfour to develop Durie Foundry, which had been established by their respective fathers. James, son of James Anderson and Agnes Gilchrist, was Provost of Leven for ten years from 1878, and was three times Captain of Leven Golf Club and a long-time member of Leven Curling Club. He was instrumental in having the Mercat Cross restored in 1889. His sisters, Agnes, Margaret, and Anne Jane, lived next door in Hawkslaw House, now Hawkslaw Hotel.

Arden House, 1986. Originally called Parkhill House, this was owned by William Wallace, a carter, whose brother, John, farmed at Balgrummo. John Wallace was married to Rachel Swan of Kettle and it was their family, Rachel, Janet and Andrew, who lived in Parkhill House in 1881. Later it was home to George Adamson, who owned Glebefield aerated water works and was a Leven Burgh Provost.

Linnwood Hall, c.1950. In 1947 Charles Carlow's son, Augustus, gave Linnwood Hall as a convalescent home to be used by miners' wives and women colliery workers. It was sold in 1970 and became a residential school for young people with severe emotional and behavioural problems. It recently housed Fife Council's Off-Campus project, aimed at getting pupils who had dropped out of mainstream schooling back into the classroom. When that moved to the Sandy Brae Centre, Kennoway, in 2000, Linnwood Hall was put up for sale.

Mason's Hall, Manse Place, 1985. The foundation stone for the new Masonic and Volunteer Hall was laid in 1896 by Major F.T. Wallace, a prime mover in having it built. In 1900 residents objected to disturbances at some 'dancings and weddings' there. Summer visitors, who looked for quietness in the nearby cottages, were disgusted as pandemonium reigned and no policeman could be found. It was later discovered that both policemen were in the hall!

Forbes Thomson Wallace, c. 1890. F.T. Wallace, brother of Michael, the Shorehead draper, was born in Buckhaven in 1840. Following the crash of the Western Bank in 1857, he became an accountant under Andrew Wilkie at the Royal Bank, on the corner of Bank Street and High Street (now the TSB) where he remained all his life. He was among the first to enrol in the 8th Leven Battery of Fife Artillery Volunteers. Along his funeral route in January 1900, businesses were shut and house blinds drawn, while several thousand people respectfully lined the streets.

David Malcolm Allan, early 1900s. D. Malcolm Allan owned two shops at 80 and 80a High Street, opposite the Caledonian Hotel. He subsequently bought and had demolished the early eighteenth century white building on the corner of High Street and North Street, replacing it in 1909 with a new building, shown below right, designed by Leven architect A.C. Dewar. This became 'Malcolm's Stationery Salon and Expeditious Newsagency' while his former shops were set aside for his 'Drapery Emporium'. He was also involved that year as Honorary Secretary, in the reforming of the Leven Golf Club.

A First World War postcard, posted in 1916. Although presented as a patriotic card during the war, the picture had actually been taken soon after D. Malcolm Allan's shop was built in 1909. The Caledonian Hotel, left, one of the oldest coaching inns in Scotland, was known in the mid-1800s as the Commercial Hotel, when George Crawford was the innkeeper. In 1836 there were twenty-eight establishments licensed to sell spirits and ales in Leven.

Caledonian Hotel, 1985. The extra storey and bay windows were added to the Caledonian Hotel in the 1930s when Robert Simpson was the proprietor. This building caught fire in the evening of 12 February 1986 and was later demolished, to be replaced by the new Caledonian Hotel now occupying the site.

The Co-operative Society had this building erected in 1909 to the plans of Mr Dow, architect, Kirkcaldy. On the ground floor were four shops, while on the upper floor were the board room and offices and behind the main building was an extensive bakery with four draw plate ovens and a Scotch oven. A courtyard was built at the back to help ease the loading of vans, and the building was extended in 1937. Following the closure of the Co-operative, the buildings, which are listed, were converted into flats around 1996, retaining most of the outer shell. In spring 2000, the Co-operative Society returned to Leven, taking over the Somerfield Store at Hawkslaw.

Scoonie Kirk, *c.*1900. The remains of the old Scoonie Kirk form the Christie burial crypt in Scoonie Cemetery. By 1760 the old building was neither wind nor water tight, but a proposal to build a new church nearer the town was proving controversial. After further deterioration, in February 1769, the congregation moved to an old barn where they worshipped for six years. The church above opened on the present site in July 1775 and, owing to the rapid increase in population, was extended in 1822 to seat 1,000.

Scoonie Kirk, 1904. By 1901 the church was again too small and the present church, seating 1,210, was erected on the same site. Designed by P. MacGregor Chalmers, Glasgow, it cost £5,200. £3,600, including £1,000 from the heritors, was raised by subscription and the balance was almost cleared by a bazaar held over three days in April 1905. The dedication ceremony took place on Saturday 6 August 1904. The church is a listed building.

East Window, Scoonie Church, *c.*1906. A.S. Cunningham said in 1905, 'Since the opening of the church, several windows have been filled in with stained glass by friends who have for years taken a practical interest in church life in Scoonie.' The east window was the work of Percy Bacon & Brothers, Edinburgh.

War Memorial Durie Street, Leven.

War Memorial, *c.*1921. The ornate iron fence was removed during the Second World War. After 1945 the names of those in Scoonie Parish who lost their lives in the most recent conflict were recorded on commemorative plaques on a semicircular wall behind the Memorial.

St John's Church, Durie Street, 1905. In 1830, Dissenters in Leven who had sympathies with the Relief Church met to form a congregation, and within two years had a church built in Viewforth Square, behind the old salt works. In 1870, during Revd John Hyslop's ministry, they built this church in Durie Street. Taking the name St John's at the Union with the Free Church in 1900, it remained this until 1975 when the congregation joined that of Forman to become St Andrew's Church. The church shown is now St Peter's RC Church and is a listed building.

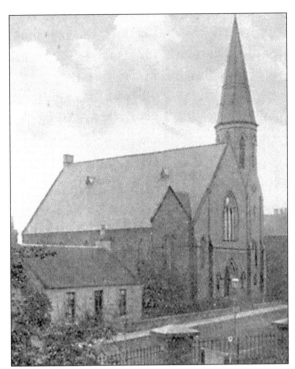

Carlow Memorial Hall, 1925. Charles Carlow, a member of St John's UF Church, generously bore much of the cost of the installation of the church organ, became an elder in 1882, and also served as Preses and Sunday School Superintendent. This hall, built by A. McRuvie and Son, was given by Charles Carlow's family to St John's Church and opened on 19 March 1925. It is a listed building.

Leven Town Hall, c.1909. In May 1843 a major row erupted in the Established Church of Scotland because congregations were not allowed to choose their ministers – this honour was in the patronage of the local laird. In the Disruption which followed, Dr George Brewster, Scoonie Kirk minister, remained with the Established Church, while the majority of the session, including the Laird of Durie, left with many of the congregation. The resulting Free Church had the church above built in December 1843, on a site provided by the Laird of Durie in Mitchell Street. In 1861 when they moved to their new Durie Street Church (later Forman) this building became the Town Hall, then 'the Jubilee'.

Forman Church, c.1900. Following the Disruption, the Revd Adam Forman, who had left the Established Church, preached on the 'face of a brae' near Innerwick, Dunbar, before receiving a call from the new Free Church in Leven. He was minister at both the above churches from 1844 until his death in 1865. This church in Durie Street was built in 1861 during his ministry and was later named Forman UF Church in his memory, becoming St Andrew's Church in 1975, at the union of St John's and Forman congregations. It is now a listed building.

Bain Hall, St Andrew's Church, 2000. David Bain, draper, of Bellevue Cottage, regarded the system of patronage as intolerable and, on moving to Leven from Kirkcaldy at the time of the Disruption, joined in the struggle of the Free Church. On his death in 1902, aged eighty-five, he was the last surviving subscriber to the original church in Mitchell Street. In 1897 he gifted this hall, now a listed building, to the Free Church.

St Margaret's Episcopal Church, c.1912. This church's missionary work began in Lundin Links in March 1861. On Christmas Day 1862, the headquarters moved to the Gardener's Hall, Murray Place, Leven. St Margaret's Church, erected on the corner of Waggon Road and Victoria Road, was consecrated by Bishop Wordsworth in August 1881. The tower was gifted by Sir Henry Gibson Carmichael of Stirling, a descendent of the Gibsons of Durie and is now a listed building.

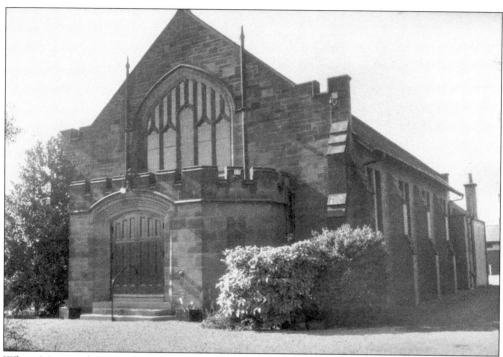

White Memorial Baptist Church, 2000. The Baptist congregation, formed in Leven in 1893, met in an iron chapel in Forth Street until this church opened in Church Road in 1913. Designed by A.C. Dewar, it was paid for by a legacy from ex-Provost John White and his sister, Jeannie. John White had inherited the lucrative brick and tile business from Alexander, his father, and retired at an early age to devote himself to public service. This is a listed building.

Commercial Road, 1985. The Hall near 'The Priory', Murray Place, was the temporary home of several religious organisations: Dissenters from September 1830 for two years, St Margaret's Episcopal Mission from 1862 for eighteen years, and latterly the Christian Brethren. 'The Priory' was also at one time a 'School for Young Ladies'. The Cornerstone Centre and Night Shelter for the Homeless are there now.

Greig Institute, 1905. This was named after Thomas Greig of Glencarse, Perthshire, since he provided the Forth Street site. Officially opened by Mr Greig on 14 July 1874, its purpose was to provide education and recreation. In 1902 it was judged to be unpopular with Leven young people as young women were not allowed to sit in the reading rooms beside the men!

Mercat Cross, 1985. In 1889, James Anderson Jnr of Norton House discovered fragments of the original Mercat Cross embedded in the gateway and garden wall of James Wilkie's house, near the Greig Institute, and with his permission, indeed help, the wall was taken down and the stones removed. After consultation with Mr Ross, an Edinburgh architect and expert on the obelisk dials of Scotland, Mr Dewar, the Leven architect, modelled the new cross on the one at Kelburne, Ayrshire, thought to most resemble the original Leven Cross. This is now in Carberry House grounds, but a replica of the cross has been made by sculptor John Thomson as part of a millennium project, and erected in School Lane where the planned Leven Tourist route will pass.

Silverburn House, 1988. George Russell moved from Collessie to farm at Hatton and, in 1854, his youngest son David, aged twenty-four, leased Silverburn Estate and had Silverburn House rebuilt. Following several industrial ventures, David joined his brother-in-law, William Tullis, at Rothes Papermill, Markinch. He married Janet, daughter of Robert Hutchison, the Kirkcaldy corn and grain merchant and in 1974 their grandson, Major David Russell, gifted Silverburn House and Estate to Leven Town Council and the National Trust.

Silverburn Cottages, c.1920. Silverburn Estate was originally bought and leased to David by his brother, Arthur, a Cupar banker. David's other industrial undertakings, at the Largo oil mills and the Burntisland sugar mill, involved seed crushing and manufacture of linseed oil and cotton cake on a big scale. The cottages above would have been built for the workers at his nearby Silverburn flax mill.

Three
Employment

In the earlier part of the nineteenth century many people worked on the land or were employed as hand loom weavers. However, as the century progressed new manufacturing industries began to dominate the economy.

Hawkslaw Spinning Mills, during the First World War, when they employed around 800 people. Fishing nets were also manufactured at Hawkslaw, which helped to provide continuous employment when the spinning industry was going through hard times. William Lindsay Boase, Binrock, Dundee, became involved with Hawkslaw Mills in 1876 as Small and Boase, running the operation in tandem with his other two Dundee works. In 1886 it became the Boase Spinning Company Ltd and later incorporated the Riverside Mills. William's maternal grandfather, William Lindsay, was a former Dundee Provost, while his father, Charles, managed the family's 'New Bank' before it amalgamated with the Dundee Banking Company and then with the Royal Bank in 1864. Hawkslaw has now been divided into small industrial units, occupied by various tradespeople.

Silverburn Flax Works, 1988. These were established by David Russell and roofed with a revolutionary new material, 'corrugated iron'. Increasingly flax was being imported, due to the reluctance of local farmers to grow it because its cultivation was thought to exhaust the soil. During the Crimean War, however, when it could not be imported from Russia, flax made a reappearance. The delicate blue bells dangling in the fields and on carts on their way to the mills 'were a sight to behold'.

Millfield Paper Mill, 1980s. In July 1888, William Grosset, who had previously been a papermaker in Lasswade and in Balbirnie Mill, Markinch, feued from Christie of Durie over three acres of land and a mill, where he established Millfield Paper Mills. He lived in Glenlyon House and ran the mill for many years with his sons, Philip, William and Alexander: the company was acquired by Fife Paper Mills in 1918. In 1989 the buildings were demolished in a road-widening scheme.

Durie Foundry, 1905. Durie Foundry continued to be run by James Anderson Jnr of Norton, and Robert and Henry Thomas Balfour, sons of the founders. Henry Thomas Balfour established an agency in London, but Robert died in 1863, aged thirty-seven. The workforce increased from forty-eight in 1835 to 240 by 1905. Having started as general engineers, the company later reached the foremost ranks of gas engineers, furnishing plant and equipment at home and overseas. They had a share in the control of the Enamelled Metal Products Corporation (1933) Ltd, who made glass-lined equipment. Pflauder-Balfour Ltd still operate from the Durie Foundry site.

Old Mill on the Leven

Leven Mills, Elm Park, 1907. These had been in the Balfour family – unrelated to the foundry family – since 1813. At first there was a sawmill and a bone mill, and when a spinning mill, added later, closed in 1848, it was converted into a linseed crushing mill, making oil cake. Cousins, John Balfour, Elm Park, and Alexander Inglis, Hawthornbank, Links, both one-time Provosts of Leven, were the works' manufacturers at the beginning of the twentieth century.

James Donaldson, *c*.1880s. By 1870, James Donaldson of Tayport was recognized as one of the leading east-coast importers of timber and his company was fast becoming one of the largest in Fife. The firm became known as James Donaldson & Sons when sons, James and George, were made partners. Tayport had been an excellent site, but increasingly their best customers were in West Fife, due to the expansion of the mining industry and their need for vast quantities of timber for the pit bottoms. A site was acquired near the new docks at Methil; nearer to the customers, it also had access to good transport facilities.

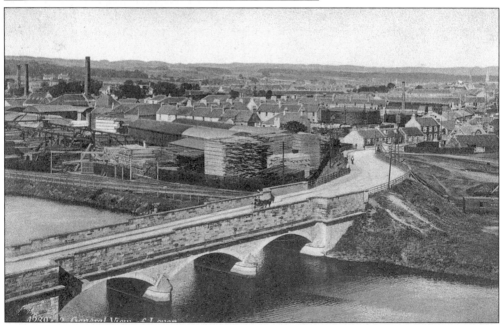

Wemyss Sawmills, 1905. They bought surplus ground close to the banks of the River Leven from the North British Railway Company and built a sawmill equipped with modern machinery and an office building. Wemyss Sawmills were hardly complete when James, the founder, suddenly died in 1891. Of James' sons, James looked after the operations at Tayport, while George was responsible for the Sawmill at Leven.

Methil Docks, c.1930. Work practices were highly labour-intensive. It was a case of 'all hands on deck' when a ship came in. Timber was handed down from the ship to the shore and then on to the waiting wagons to the yard where they would be unloaded and stacked again, all by hand. This cargo was about to be transported to the Leven Mill.

Directors, Administrative and Management Staff, Centenary Year, 1960. James Donaldson & Sons still operate at Elm Park, although the original Wemyss Sawmill site was sold in 1997 to Sainsbury for a supermarket. Head Office is now at Haig Business Park, Markinch, and Neil Donaldson, Managing Director, is the fifth generation in a line of eldest sons to run the company. In June 2000, George Donaldson, Chairman, third from right, front row, was awarded a CBE in the Queen's birthday honours list, for his services to the timber industry.

Bon Accord Works, Parkhill, 1986. Holidaymakers and residents in Leven were spoilt for choice for local 'aerated water'. At the end of the nineteenth century, Alex Marshall operated in Waggon Road, while Christopher Adamson had his works in Glebefield. On the Bon Accord Work's roof can be seen the name of previous tenant, Andrew Hutchison, whose family firm manufactured aerated water there from the First World War until 1972. (He also operated a coach building business next door from 1938.)

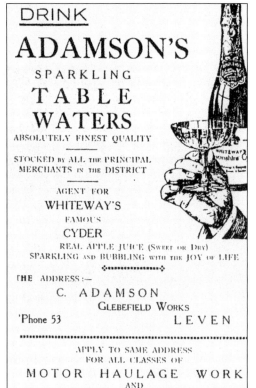

This was the 'opposition' in Glebefield, off Durward Street. Begun by Christopher Adamson of Trinity Place, it was continued by his son, George W. Adamson, after his father's death in 1912. Both were Provosts of the Burgh of Leven, Christopher during the period 1903-1906, and George from 1924-1927. George, who lived in Parkhill House, died in 1963, aged seventy-seven.

Four

Summer Resort

The coming of the railway to Leven in 1854 was instrumental in the town's growth as a holiday resort. In the nineteenth century only affluent people would have residential seaside holidays but, as the twentieth century progressed, these were enjoyed by all classes of society.

Leven Sands, 1907. Seaside holidays were regarded as 'healthy' and sprang primarily from the tradition of 'taking the waters' at inland spas. However, a combination of parliamentary reforms granting statutory holidays and the issuing of special excursion tickets by the railway companies, brought a new attitude to holidays by the seaside. Children, previously excluded from 'health visits' to the coast, joined in the family seaside holidays, thereby spawning the tradition of buckets and spades, building sandcastles and generally having fun on the sands.

Promenade, *c.*1900. This view looking west from Innerleven Golf Clubhouse shows the rough road and sand dunes on the Promenade at that time. In their efforts to have the town ready for the influx of visitors in 1900, the Town Council proposed to have in place six seats between Scoonie Burn and the River Leven by the summer when the beach road 'would be nearly done'.

Promenade, *c.*1903. In the period when only the well-to-do visited resorts like Leven, houses would be rented for families and their servants for several months during the summer. These fine villas, complete with upper verandas, were built in the closing years of the nineteenth century.

Promenade, *c.*1910. By then, Leven had become a paradise for trippers. A proper road had at last been constructed between the villas and the Links, and visitors and locals were entertained by 'artistes' from specially-constructed stages. In addition to golf and bowling, there was a Swimming Club and a Lawn Tennis Club. Another popular attraction was Madame Roma, an expert in palmistry who visited Leven regularly. Tea could be taken at the Promenade Tea Rooms.

Promenade, *c.*1917. Donkey rides and the ice-cream cart had arrived! Summer visitors were entertained on the Links by the Town Band, trained by band instructor, C. Marsden. Criticisms were made that the Swimming Clubhouse was situated at a nasty part of the beach, too near the River Leven, and that some means would have to be devised to overcome the inconvenience of having to dress on the sands!

PUTTING GREEN, LEVEN.

Promenade, c.1926. Improvements on the Promenade, carried out by the Town Council in the 1920s, included the construction of a new road between Scoonie Burn and the salmon bothy, and the laying out of the putting green above. In 1926 a new 'Pierrot Pavilion' was being planned and, the following year, the entertainer's stage on the right was replaced by a pavilion.

THE BEACH CONCERT HALL, AND PROMENADE, LEVEN.

Beach Concert Hall, c.1927. The official opening was held on the 4 June 1927. In order to avoid confusion with the Town Hall Pavilion, the Town Council decided to change the name of the new building from 'Beach Pavilion' to 'Beach Concert Hall'. The hall could seat 800 people and was leased to entertainers in the summer and to the Badminton Club in the winter.

Promenade, 1920s. The Town Council feued the beach from the Laird of Durie Estate for £100 a year, giving them control of the beach from the River Leven in the west to the Scoonie Burn in the east, and to the high water mark in the south. In this picture, the Merry Mascots were entertaining, while there was a marquee opposite on ground which became the Festival Gardens in 1953. Travelling circuses had been a popular feature on the Links since the late nineteenth century.

Promenade, c.1926. Having won the right to vote, then subsequently discovered their worth in the workplace during the war, women in the 1920s became more self-assured and turned their attention to fashion. Two stylish ladies of the period stopped to chat on 'Leven Esplanade'.

Leven Golfing Society Clubhouse. Golf was played on Dubbieside Links in the middle of the eighteenth century and Innerleven Golfing Society was formed around 1820. In 1867, when railway sidings encroached on Dubbieside Links, the Innerleven Club crossed the River Leven and joined with the Leven Club on 'the popular green' between Scoonie Burn and Mile Dyke. The Innerleven Club had their clubhouse – now Thistle Clubhouse – built around 1883, then had this grand building erected in 1894.

Members of Leven Golf Club, 1857, taken by J. Patrick, photographer. From left, John Patrick, a cabinet maker who began making golf clubs in a shop in Branch Street in 1847; Alexander Patrick, his son who left school in 1857 to join his father in business and later became a famous club maker; Robert Bruce, tailor, -?-, William Robertson, William Wallace, carter, Parkhill House, John Davidson, David Malcolm, shoemaker, Alexander Sibbald, ? Guthrie, Matthew Elder, rope and twine manufacturer, Dr Cornfoot, Robert Smith, Shorehead draper, Peter Keddie, saddler, three boys (not known) and William Henderson. The club, formed in 1847, lapsed in 1884 but was later reconstituted. In 1958, however, they joined the Innerleven Club to become the Leven Golfing Society.

Leven Thistle Golf Clubhouse and Scoonie Burn, c.1904. The Thistle Golf Club was formed in 1867. Without a clubhouse for many years, they firstly acquired some wooden structure, then rented another building before finally taking possession in 1895 of the former Innerleven Clubhouse. They completed an extension in 1900 and the Thistle soon became popular with 'all classes of the community'.

Innerleven and Thistle Golf Clubhouses, 1910. Within a year of the Innerleven Club moving from Dubbieside Links, Leven's nine hole course, from Scoonie Burn to the Mile Dyke, was extended to Lundin Mill, the first competition on the eighteen-hole course taking place in September 1868. Sir John Gilmour later terminated Innerleven's lease of the course between Mile Dyke and Lundin Links, but the Club then leased ground which included the stretch of links which for years had formed the Leven Ladies Golf Course.

The Beach Hotel, c.1958. This was the only hotel on the Promenade. In the late 1980s, disturbances following weekend functions at the hotel became a source of irritation to local residents. After a serious fire in 1989, the hotel was demolished and the Beach Nursing Home was built on the site in around 1993.

Caravan Park, c.1960. In 1953, the Town Council Beach Committee called their caravan site to the east of the Salmon Bothy, 'Shepherd's Knowe'. Forty caravans could be parked there, and were charged 2s 6d per day or 12s 6d per week. The Caravan Park was sold by the Council in 1990 and is now called 'Leven Beach Holiday Park' which has over 100 residential caravans and can accommodate sixteen touring vans.

Letham Glen, c.1940. The Town Council feued Spinkie Den – spinkie being the Scots word for primrose – from the Laird of Durie. Interest on a gift of £1,000 from retired farmer, John Letham, helped offset the cost and in appreciation 'Spinkie Den' became 'Letham Glen'. A swimming pool was constructed by miners through a scheme devised to relieve unemployment, and a putting green was laid out. Jack Ashwood's 'Merrymakers' opened on 19 June 1925. The entrance gates are now listed.

'Leo and Edna', c.1928. Harry Fraser, Abbotsford, and Edna Smith, Burghlea, were neighbours in Waggon Road. As 'Leo and Edna', they entered a 'go as you please' competition run by Jack Ashwood in Letham Glen, where Harry had helped to erect the gates and railings, forged at the family's 'Parkhill Smiddy'. 'Leo and Edna' toured many Scottish towns, accompanied by pianist Jimmy Kidd. Harry married Rebecca Smith and in 1949 they emigrated to Australia where Rebecca died in 1974. Harry lives with his second wife, Lois, in Noosaheads, Queensland.

Trinity House, *c*.1920s. William R. Bisset began decorating his home, Trinity House, Seagate, with shells as a hobby and, after opening it to the public in around 1927, it quickly became a major Leven attraction. Every summer as many as 30,000 people visited the 'Buckie House'. An article about it even appeared in the New York Journal.

Buckie Bus, *c*.1934. The project was continued by his son, James. A Leyland bus, encrusted with shells, and a small animal zoo were added attractions. When James died in 1978, the enterprise was regarded as uneconomic and a buyer could not be found. Following the demolition of the 'Buckie Bus', a bungalow was built on the site.

Five

Methil, Buckhaven and Methilhill

Three very different villages, Innerleven, Buckhaven and Methil were formed into a Police Burgh in May 1891, becoming the Burgh of Buckhaven, Methil and Innerleven, although the latter name has been dropped over the years. Methilhill, an old mining village, was rebuilt as a model town in 1924 for the employees of the Wemyss Coal Company.

Innerleven, c.1905. In pre-Reformation times when there was a priory at Markinch, the hamlet of Innerleven (or Dubbieside), being at the mouth of the River Leven, was chosen to supply the monks with fresh fish, so the village was part of Markinch Parish until 1891 when it joined Wemyss Parish. Traditional industries were fishing and weaving. Many Dissenters left the official Church of Scotland in the eighteenth century and, after belonging to the Ceres and Abbotshall Presbyteries, acquired their own church in Dubbieside in the 1790s. For many years their minister, the Revd John Macdonald from Ireland, brought thousands of people to worship on the banks of the River Leven at his open-air tent meetings, the type satirized by Robert Burns in his 'Holy Fair'.

Kirkland Bridge, 1907. Although this looks a picturesque spot, at one time forty industrial works operated on the river between Leslie and Leven and, in the early 1900s, pollution levels at Kirkland were particularly bad; salmon and trout had deserted the river. Due to recent strict environmental controls, salmon, trout and sea-trout have returned to the river and, when the new waste water treatment plant is operational, water quality on the river and in the estuary will be much improved.

Kirkland Village, c.1900. Coal mining at Kirkland ceased in 1785 and was succeeded by linen manufacturing, flax spinning and bleaching. Kirkland Works were the second largest on the River Leven, employing about 800 people. The transition from handloom to powerloom had been very successful there, but the effect of cheap imported goods eventually led to bankruptcy and closure in 1882. The houses of the workers formed a large village where miners, labourers, carters and firemen lived when this picture was taken beside the village well.

Crossroads, early 1900s. The large white building behind the fireman with the horse and cart was the Kirkland Branch of the Leven Reform Co-operative Society. As well as the cottages on the left, villagers lived in Dryburgh's Buildings, Young's buildings and Rose's Buildings. The open countryside beyond the Co-operative was farmed by James and Archibald Dalrymple of Kirkland Hill Farm, now the office of Sinclair and Watt, architects, Den Walk.

Crossroads, c.1905. The old chapel school of St Agatha's, right, was used during the week as a school while on Sundays it served as the church. The building was demolished following subsidence caused by old pit workings, and a new St Agatha's School was later built on the site. On adjoining ground the present St Agatha's RC Church, designed by Reginald Fairlie, opened on 28 August 1923. On the left was the Headmaster's house and Crossroads Public School, opened in 1875 when George Mathieson was headmaster, and extended in 1887. This school was also demolished due to subsidence and Woodlands Nursery now stands on that site.

Braefoot, Methil, *c.*1910. The stylish 'Turret House' belonged to Alexander Wilson, a retired vintner, while on the ground floor was the shop of William Low and Co. Ltd. The tin church of the Rechabite Order – a teetotal organization – can be identified by the slim, pointed spire, midway up the section of Methil Brae shown here. The Railway Bar belonged to Adam Stewart.

High Street, Methil, *c.*1908. In 1905 Adam Stewart of the Railway Bar bought land from Christian Andreas Gottfried Fyhn, the local ship's chandler, and built this fine building, on the right, which he called the National Bar. He sold it in 1914 to James Stein, Vintner, Penang House, Methil, and retired to Wemyssfield, Kirkcaldy.

No.2 Dock, Methil, c.1902. Mr R.G.E. Wemyss had a new dock constructed at Methil in 1887, following guarantees from his tenant coal companies, Messrs Bowman and Company and the Fife Coal Company, that they would ship a fixed tonnage of coal annually. The Thornton to Methil Railway opened simultaneously and, having sold both dock and railway within a year to the North British Railway Company, Mr Wemyss agitated for a second dock to be built. Dock No.2, partially opened in 1897, was completed in 1899.

Main Street, Methil, 1908. Methil had a Main Street as well as a High Street. Business premises in the foreground included those of William Carrie, solicitor; the Wemyss Arms, with the decorative lamp at No.62, which was run by Elizabeth Lindsay, while Thomas Ballingall was the grocer at No.58.

Methil. Has long possessed commercial importance in consequence of its Harbour being one of the best on the south coast of Fife. It is yearly growing in importance.

View from the Shepherd's Park, *c.*1905. Methil Golf Club, whose first President was Provost Greig, was founded in 1892. They secured the Shepherd's Park as a course, having six holes for the first four years, then extending it to nine. It soon began to be encroached upon by railway lyes and houses, however, and by 1903 it was abandoned, like Dubbieside, and Leven Links were made the club's headquarters.

In 1906 Messrs J.C. Rolland, A. Robertson, R. Goodall and W. White of Methil Golf Club had the distinction of winning the Fife County Championship Trophy, presented to Fife Clubs by the proprietors of the *Evening Telegraph and Post*.

The Docks, Methil.

No.3 Dock, Methil, 1914. Methil had been for many years the greatest coal shipping port in Scotland and a third dock, built on the site of the old Dubbieside links, opened on 22 January 1913. Following pit closures in the late twentieth century, insufficient volume of trade necessitated the closure in 1977 of No.3 Dock, which was filled in and turned into an industrial estate. 'New Bayview', East Fife Football Club's stadium, has been built there.

High Street, Methil.

High Street, Methil, c.1923. On the right of this picture was James Robertson's stationer's shop at No.7, next door to the Maypole Dairy Company, with its globe lights, at No.9. At No.11 was William Ness, fish merchant, while on the opposite side of the road was Dewar's Fish Restaurant.

'Old Buckhaven', early 1900s, painted by Alexander Young. The fishermen from Buckhaven, or Buckhyne, took part in the 'Winter Herring' from December to March in the Firth of Forth. During the 'Summer Drave', from June to August, Buckhaven fishermen and fisher lassies followed the herring to their favoured port of North Shields. They would then leave in September for Yarmouth, returning in November. In 1855, 500 men and boys earned their living as crew in the fleet of 168 boats which then belonged to Buckhaven.

Early 1900s. Andrew Kirkcaldy was carrying his wooden small line scull in which he would arrange his line and hooks for easy handling. The small lines were used for fishing near the shore, in small boats with three or four crew, each man having a 300ft line, attached to which would be 100 snoods carrying the baited hooks. Each line was laid in a scull so it could be run out cleanly as the boat went along. In 1881, Andrew lived at East End, Buckhyne with his family.

Hynehead, Buckhaven c.1920. The fishermen's houses in Buckhaven had been described as miserable and as resembling seabirds' nests on a shore cliff. The entry in Chamber's Edinburgh Journal of 1833, however, says that they were built in that way because of the scantiness of the ground originally allotted to people who needed to occupy every site on which a house could stand. Each house was described as being decently furnished with a neat oaken table and chairs, a chest of drawers, an eight-day clock and a large well-bound quarto Bible.

Buckhaven, c.1900. When husbands fished locally in the Firth of Forth, their wives dried the nets for their return. The women's day might begin at four o' clock in the morning when they would bait the lines, assisted by some older children who would shell the mussels. While baiting the lines, she might rock the newest family member by having a string tied from a cradle to her foot. More than a thousand hooks were baited on every line and this was regarded in Scotland as women's work. Spare time would be spent mending nets or knitting.

Hyne Rocks, Buckhaven, 1906. Children would be absent from school to help their fathers prepare the boats prior to their departure for North Shields or Yarmouth, and similarly they would not attend school if the boats were due to return. These children were on the Hyne rocks, which would later be completely covered by the 'redd', or waste, from Wellesley Colliery.

FATHER'S BOAT.

Early 1900s. Children watched eagerly for their fathers' boats returning and could tell at some distance whose boat it was by a new mast, or by the distinctive mark of the fish curer for whom their fathers had agreed to work. Buckhaven fishwives in their blue costumes travelled many miles inland with their heavy baskets of fish and were almost as famous as those of Newhaven or Fisherrow. (The local fishermen liked to wear red cowls.)

Andrew Thomson, born 1810, Buckhaven. In Buckhaven in 1833, there were 160 families, but only about a dozen surnames. Seventy-two families of Thomson topped the list by a long way. To distinguish one Thomson from another (and likewise other surnames), bye names were used, such as the name of the skipper's ship, his wife's name or some unusual physical attribute. In 1877, among boat owners in Buckhaven there were three Andrew Thomson's. Andrew Thomson (Alliance), Andrew Thomson (Elizabeth) and Andrew Thomson (Eminent).

Agenora (ML 53) Crew, 1895. 'Arles' was money paid in advance, as a type of contract, to boat crews and fisher girls by curing firms who would employ them when they reached their fishing port. The curers came to Buckhaven to sign them up before they left for North Shields or Yarmouth. After settling in for the season, the boat crews and fisher girls used their 'arles' to pay to have their picture taken, to send home to the families. Back row, left to right: James Thomson, James Taylor, William Thomson (son of Andrew above) Front row: James Gordon, Thomas Thomson, Walter Foster and Robert Thomson (owner).

Buckhaven harbour, c.1918. Buckhaven fishermen formed an association in around 1822 to raise money to add to the Fishery Board's grant, in order to build a harbour. Built in 1838 and extended in 1853, the harbour eventually became silted up by the 'redd' from the Wellesley Colliery. During a storm in 1937, a breach of about 40 yards appeared in the East Pier, leaving the entrance blocked by the debris. The lighthouse, which had become isolated, collapsed in a storm in 1942.

Buckhaven lifeboat, *Isabella*, early 1900s. In 1900 a lifeboat station was established and a lifeboat house and slipway (centre of top picture) were constructed at the harbour head. The lifeboat, of the 'Liverpool' type, was a legacy from Miss Isabella Haxton of Kirkcaldy. It was launched on a wheeled cradle and released in deeper water. The *Isabella* was sold in 1932 to a gentleman in South Queensferry, who used it as a pleasure cruiser. Latterly it sailed between Gourock and Greenock.

West High Street, c.1900. A fisherman's house, right, can be distinguished by the hoist which would have been used to take his fishing gear directly into the loft. West High Street was the dividing line between the fishing community and those engaged in other industries up the town. Intermarriage between fisher folk and folk 'up the toon' was discouraged since a fisherman needed a wife who would be able to shell the mussels, bait the lines and mend nets among other things.

Buckhaven area, c.1910. Lawson's Dairy used to be in East High Street, so perhaps this was taken there. Today's environmental health officers would not be impressed, but this was once a common sight! Another country custom involved countrywomen taking their surplus butter to local markets; in order to keep it cool they would wrap it in a rhubarb leaf, or immerse it for a time in a well.

Lawrence Street, Buckhaven, *c.*1905. As the old fishing houses fell into disrepair, people moved to smart cottages and villas 'up the toon'. Summer visitors found comfortable lodgings in these houses as Buckhaven became a popular summer resort.

Church Street, Buckhaven , *c.*1905. This corner of Church Street had for years been a scene of animation at fairs and holiday times. Building began on this church in 1884, but during a violent gale the front gable was blown down. Named Muiredge Church, as it was situated on Muiredge Farm ground, it opened on 2 July 1885, while the manse was built in 1902. Regarded as a 'daughter' of St David's Church, these two congregations united in 1939.

Thomson's Net Factory, Buckhaven, early 1920s. In 1840 William Thomson set up a new net factory in Randoph Street, employing forty workers. They produced cotton drift nets, superior to the twine ones since they caught more herring. Irvine of Glasgow took it over in 1924, but net making ceased in 1945. They were followed by Watson's oilskin factory, Randolph Leisurewear's clothing factory, then the Buckhaven Parish Church Agency. The latter folded in 1991 and in 1994 the building was demolished and two houses were built on the site.

M. Warrender, c.1914. In this picture of a local girl on the Braes, the chimney of the net factory can be seen 'up the hill'.

Randolph Street, Buckhaven c.1912. There was an influx of families into Buckhaven in 1882, many taking possession of new houses in Randolph Street. The local school admitted 325 new pupils and it was recorded that they were 'deficient in education'. Many of the shops in Randolph Street were owned by Buckhaven Co-operative Society.

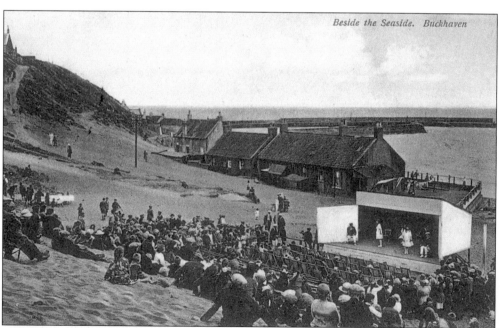

Ness Braes, Buckhaven, c.1925. During one weekend in July 1925, 3,000 visitors arrived in Buckhaven to enjoy family fun on the golden sands. Pierrots provided beach entertainment on the Ness Braes or 'Happy Valley'. Every Sunday different types of bands, with renowned soloists, enthralled large crowds for hours at a time. The Promenade was at the front of these cottages; the end of it can be seen above the entertainer's hut.

Church Street, Buckhaven, *c*.1955. Supermarkets had not yet arrived. The Co-operative Society in nearby Randolph Street, as well as their travelling vans, provided most necessities for the neighbourhood and was the most important retail outlet in the community. Small independent businesses like these on the left were also invaluable to local people in an age when many families did not yet own a car.

An advert from 1960. On 14 March 1952, the Kirk O' Shotts transmitter opened and television had arrived in the area. Public demonstrations were given in halls, hotels and pubs; around 150-200 people attended one in St Michael's Church Hall. As well as the Co-operative Society, R.S. Nicol, College Street, was a local dealer. In pubs the customers' eyes were glued to the screen and the local Leven Mail reporter said they asked for their pints in a whisper; he wondered how long the new toy would prove popular in these places! Soon 'X' and 'H' shaped aerials appeared on chimneys everywhere. Only one BBC channel was available at first, then around 1957 came ITV and advertisements.

Methilhill, 1932. The old mining village of Methilhill consisted of a few rows of small houses: Ivy Row, Irish Row, Brick Row, Cottar Row and Attic Row. Most were replaced by the fine houses of the model mining village built in 1924. My grandparents were the first tenants at 10 Brown Crescent before moving later to 4 Mathieson Place, from where this picture was taken. The author's grandfather, Tom Nicolson, died that year from bronchopneumonia, to which many miners succumbed due to their adverse working conditions.

Methilhill Church, c.1931. Methilhill Church was impressively designed by Peter Sinclair, taking the shape of a crucifix. It was built of brick and sandstone by Forrester and Son, Leven; the pulpit and woodwork were of Austrian oak and the joiner was D. Dewar, Methil. Vast crowds attended the opening on Saturday 4 April 1931 when the sermon was preached by Assembly Moderator, the Right Revd A.N. Bogle, DD. Minister of the Church was Mr McKenzie, William Taylor was Session Clerk, organist was Alec McKenzie from Kettle, and James Brown was Church Officer.

Methilhill, *c*.1952. Th author's husband's parents bought a wooden hut shop at Pirnie Crossing, Methilhill, from Elizabeth 'Tibbie' Donaldson of 6 Bowhouse Place. Nessie Caldwell, right, and a member of staff are at the shop door where the board promotes Alexander's bus tours to Kirriemuir and Glamis, Pitlochry and Aberdeen, and, of course, Mystery Tours.

Methilhill, *c*.1952. Staff members, Jessie Thomson and Jenny Clarke, in front of the hut shop, where in addition to the Beechnut machine, there are advertisements for 'seven o'clock' blades and Brooke Bond tea.

Methilhill, *c*.1954. The hut shop was replaced a few years later by a brick building. Apart from the demolition of the original hut shop, the business remained as above until the 1970s when it was extended and became a VG Convenience Store.

Methilhill, 1982. This springtime picture is of Wullie Gillan who, for many years, helped to keep the village looking at its best.

Six

Mining

Following the major expansion of local coalfields in the late nineteenth and early twentieth centuries, the industry was in recent years wiped out locally due to the loss of traditional markets. Large reserves of coal still exist, and some open-cast mining is currently taking place on the border of Wemyss Parish.

COAL BEARING AND ITS DANGERS.

In Scotland until the early nineteenth century, where mines were comparatively shallow, coal was carried by women and those of their daughters considered old enough, along the pit bottom and up the stairway in the shaft to the pit mouth. The mother would set off from the pit bottom with her burden on her back, carrying a lit candle between her teeth, followed by her daughters, until they reached the top. They did this for 8 to 10 hours without rest and it was not uncommon for them to weep bitterly on their way up the ladder due to the excessive weight. They would leave for the pit in the early hours of the morning, after the mother had given over her infant, wrapped in a blanket, and her other small children to an old woman who might also, in the mother's absence, give them ale or whisky mixed with water. An Act of 1842, stating that 'miners were far better without females in the pits', put an end to this misery!

Old-style pithead, *c.*1905. Local colliery owners at the beginning of the twentieth century were the Fife Coal Company (Leven, Pirnie and Wellsgreen Pits) and Messrs Bowman and Company (Muiredge, Rosie and Denbeath Pits), the latter company being replaced by the Wemyss Coal Company in 1905, when their lease ran out. This old-style pit would be similar to Pirnie Pit and the old Denbeath.

Pit bottom, early 1900s. In March 1921, during a bitter national coal strike, safety men were withdrawn, resulting in the pits filling with water. Press publicity focused on two Leven pit ponies, drowned, it was alleged, because the men refused to allow pumping to continue. The Society for the Prevention of Cruelty to Animals was enlisted in the campaign against the miners, and one of their officials went around Buckhaven with summonses.

Old Washer, Leven Pit, 1986. In 1877 Fife Coal Company, which became Scotland's greatest coal mining concern, opened Leven Pit, Nos1 and 2, at Kinnarchie Braes, Aberhill. The coalfield was extended in 1905 to include Kirkland old coal workings. Leven Pit closed in around 1930, as it was the only company pit to continually lose money. This washer stood behind the offices of Central Farmers, who took over the site in 1933.

Aitken Place, 1960s. Streets like Carlow Place and Aitken Place, Leven, were constructed by coal companies for their workers. Coal owners wielded significant influence over their workers; if a miner lost his job, he also lost his home. On the extreme left can be seen a wash-house which was used by miners as a 'soup kitchen' during the 1926 strike.

Links of Buckhaven, *c.*1906. The Wemyss Coal Company took over the old Denbeath Pit in 1905, enlarged it and called it the Wellesley. The Baum Washer, which washed coal before sizing it, dominates this picture and below it, on the Shore Road, was Links of Buckhaven, or Links Village, midway between Buckhaven and Methil. This settlement and road were acquired by the Laird to provide land for the disposal of pit 'redd' and for sidings for the Wellesley. The Links' inhabitants were mainly rehoused in College Street, Buckhaven, and Links disappeared around 1909 below the rubble.

Wellesley Road, *c.*1906. The Laird of Wemyss built Wellesley Road, connecting Muiredge with Leven, to replace the Links Road. Between 1904 and 1908, 270 Denbeath houses built by the Wemyss Coal Company earned the name, 'The Garden City'. They housed mainly incoming miners to the Wellesley Colliery, from Lanarkshire, Ireland and elsewhere but, early on, the majority were former shale miners from the Lothians.

Wellesley Colliery, *c.*1970. The Baum Washer, an innovation from Germany, handled around 1,000 tonnes of coal a day and treated most of the Wemyss Company's coal. Wellesley Colliery, named after the Laird's second wife, Lady Eva Wellesley, employed about 2,500 people in the 1960s, but closed around 1968. Redpath Dorman Long acquired the site in 1972 to build jackets for oil platforms in the burgeoning North Sea Oil industry. (*Picture courtesy of the Scottish Mining Museum*)

Lochhead FC, 1921-1922. Football was an important leisure pursuit of miners and many were involved in amateur football leagues. Mining was hard, physical work, and young boys, aged fourteen, left school to follow their fathers and other family members underground, having to gradually build up their strength. At Lochhead Colliery coal was cut entirely by hand.

The Michael Colliery, East Wemyss, early 1960s. On 9 September 1967 a seam of coal ignited 1,800ft below ground at the Michael Colliery, which was Scotland's largest and deepest coal mine and which employed around 3,500 men. Nine men lost their lives: James Tait (41), Henry Morrison (35), Johnston Smith (60), Philip Thomson (64), Andrew Thomson (55), Alexander Henderson (41), H. Gallagher (61), J. McKay (59) and A. Taylor (43) – a fearful reminder of the danger faced by miners on a daily basis. *(Picture courtesy of the Scottish Mining Museum)*

West Wemyss Harbour, c.1900. In 1872 when the natural harbour at West Wemyss was being converted into a wet dock, the mouths of three shafts were found, and in one of them a flight of steps, forming a link with the days when women carried coal on their backs from the coal face to the surface. This harbour did a large trade in the export of coal. When this George Washington Wilson photograph was taken, however, local coal production was beginning to wane, except for that at the Lochhead and Michael Pits.

Seven
Windygates and Kennoway

Cameronbridge Distillery, Windygates, owned by United Distillers and Vintners, produces grain spirit for blended whiskies and recently became the production centre for the company's white spirits, which are bottled at their packaging plant at Banbeath, Leven. Due to recent house building, Windygates has now virtually joined up with Kennoway, which itself has dramatically increased in size since the end of the Second World War.

Hugh Veitch Haig, son of John Haig, was born at Cameron Bridge in 1844. He was a grandson of William Haig, one-time Provost of St Andrews and owner of Kincaple Maltings. Hugh and his brother William ran the family's distillery, John Haig & Co. at Cameron Bridge, which had been started by their father in 1824. Shortly before his marriage, Hugh purchased the estate of Bridgend, and it was largely due to his exertions that the large distilleries of Scotland united into the whisky organization, the Distillers' Company Ltd, in 1877. This fine mansion, Bridgend House, originally called Cameron Bridge House, was demolished following a fire in around 1990 and a housing estate was built on the site.

Cameron Bridge, Windygates, 1990. In 1854, when the railway opened, a report said, 'Close to the station is Cameron Bridge, an old narrow edifice and near it are Cameron Mills and Cameron Distillery possessed by John Haig and Co. With its smoky chimneys, granaries, distilling machinery and sheds for feeding of cattle, the distillery is a large work employing a major number of people and yielding considerable revenue to Government.' (The old bridge was to the west of the present one, which was built in 1900.)

Station Road, Windygates, c.1904. Shops in Station Road included those of Markinch Co-operative, left, John and James Rattray, Cycle Makers and Repairers, and William Brown, who had a general drapery, fancy goods and Boot and Shoe Warehouse. Further west, at 'the Meetings', Johnny Wishart, a miller, was immortalized in this rhyme. He refused to sell his 'napkin of land' for a good price so he would not lose the proverb. 'Lochrie, Lothrie, Leven and Ore– A' met at Johnny Wishart's door.'

Milton Road, Windygates, c.1903. On the right were the villas of Haughmill Lane while on the left were the old one-storey cottages. To the north of these cottages was the older and quite separate hamlet of Balcurvie, now part of the village, which at one time was mainly a community of weavers.

Windygates Cross, 1990. This clock was erected in 1916 from proceeds of the 'Social Betterment Dairy Scheme'. The government tried to persuade people to drink milk rather than alcohol as excessive drinking, particularly among munitions workers, was hampering munitions production and was having a serious effect on the war effort. A law was passed by the Lloyd George Government forbidding a man to treat a friend to a drink. Prominent notices, were displayed in public houses saying, 'No treating'.

Windygates Cross, *c*.1912. The lady in the doorway of the 'ice-cream saloon', built in 1910, was probably Carmine Nardelli, the 'ice-cream dealer'. The shop was owned later by the Gallo family. David Dunsire owned the draper's shop, left, while the shoemaker's shop on second block, right, belonged to George Murray. The Cross was a major traffic junction until a bypass was built in 1993.

Windygates Hotel, *c*.1903. Windygates was at one time the great posting station for east Fife. The posting establishment consisted of the hotel, stabling accommodation and the building on the left, which later became a stationers and newsagents before being demolished in the 1970s to relieve the traffic situation. The coming of the railway led to the demise of the posting industry. Artist, John Houston, ARSA, was a son of the family who owned this hotel.

Kennoway Burns, c.1908. Two burns, or streams, meet here – one flows from Markinch, the other from land south of Kettle. Over the original bridge, to the left of this picture, and up the 'Sandy Hole', was the picturesque way from the south to approach Kennoway village. Council houses were built on the Sandy Brae in the 1920s to rehouse families in a slum clearance scheme and in the early 1970s a housing estate was built behind the cottages on the left.

Maiden Castle, Kennoway Burns, c.1990. This prominent man-made earth mound, known as a motte, would in early medieval times have supported, on its flat-topped summit, a timber castle surrounded by a palisade fence, while a moat would have encircled the base. It would have been a residence and stronghold of a feudal lord, thought to have been MacDuff, Thane of Fife, since Hounstead in 1570 attributed ownership to 'Fifus Duffus or MacDuff'. Doubt exists, however, as to the truth of this.

Archbishop James Sharp, c.1670s. After the Restoration of the Monarchy in 1660, King Charles II and the Scottish nobility restored episcopal government to the Church of Scotland, thinking bishops would be easier to control than ministers and elders. They chose James Sharp, Minister of Crail, to be Archbishop of St Andrews. Since Sharp had been a leading member of the Resolutioners (Presbyterians), the Covenanters viewed his acceptance of this appointment as an act of betrayal and he became one of the most hated men in Scotland. When he took possession of the See in 1662, he made a triumphal progression from Leslie, the Earl of Rothes' house, to St Andrews, accompanied by 700 horsemen and the Earls of Rothes and Kellie, but only two ministers were present.

'Archbishop Sharp's house', Kennoway, early 1900s. On 3 May 1679, Kennoway villagers watched the departure of Archbishop Sharp and his daughter, Isabel, from the house of his kinsman, Captain Seton, with whom they had stayed overnight en route from Edinburgh to St Andrews. His coach and six – possibly the one he brought from London for his ceremonial entry described above, since they were rare in Scotland – emerged from the gateway to lumber noisily over the 'causey stanes' on its way to St Andrews via the bleak Magus Muir, where he was dragged from his coach and killed. This house, one of two Kennoway houses to claim the honour of this historic stay, was a seventeenth-century two-storey building, typical of the 'town houses' of the Scottish gentry of that period, possessing fine wood panelling and moulded fireplaces in both apartments. It was demolished many years ago, only the coat of arms being saved and built into a neighbouring garage.

ARCH-BISHOP SHARP'S HOUSE, KENNOWAY.

Causeway, Kennoway, c.1907. Local markets were held in April and October here beside the churchyard in the oldest part of Kennoway. The arrival of Mary Smith – with coal-scuttle straw bonnet and red shawl – was a notable event of the morning, 'from the time that the cart appeared on the brae of the Sandyhole to the putting up of the legs of the wooden stall with its canvas awning and the laying out of the gingerbread and sweets'. The custom died when trade through shops became more common.

Causewayhead, Kennoway, c.1906. The village once had fifteen or sixteen malt and brew steadings, but these ultimately failed and their buildings became ruinous. When repaired they became the homes of weavers and other trades people. This looks towards Swan Hotel, formerly Swan Inn, where J.H. Browne said, 'A small parlour was reserved for special occasions and the 'gauntry' adjoining the kitchen held the whisky barrels where a stout ruddy-faced ...woman in a mutch was now providing the party with whisky.' In 1838, thirteen establishments in the parish were licensed to sell spirits and ales.

Established Church, Kennoway, *c.*1905. The first preaching of Christianity in east Fife is attributed to St Kenneth, patron saint of Kennoway. The pre-reformation church of reeds and wattles, at the top of the Causeway, was extended and strengthened in 1619, then further extended in 1832. By 1850 it was neither wind nor waterproof, and this new building was erected on its present site at the Cross. The church hall shown was gifted by Miss Wallace, Newton Hall. The church is now known as St Kenneth's.

Established Church Manse, Kennoway *c.*1905. The Church Glebe, on which this handsome manse was built in 1833, was about seven acres. This building is now a private house and in the early 1970s a housing development was built on the remainder of the glebe.

Halfields Farm, 1985. In 1732 Revd Ebenezer Erskine, North Church, Stirling, began his campaign against the 1712 Patronage Act which had restored to local lairds and absentee landlords the right to choose the parish minister. His brother, Revd Ralph Erskine, Dunfermline, joined him and they were both expelled from the Established Church of Scotland. The anti-patronage cause was overwhelmingly strong in Fife and Kennoway villagers caused a sensation by leaving the Established Church to join the Secession Church. Ralph Erskine, a popular preacher at open-air communion gatherings, preached to these adherents in June 1738 on the sunny slopes of Halfields.

Arnot Church, Kennoway, c.1905. By 1753 the Secession Church, or Associate Presbytery, had built a church and called William Arnot from Kinross as its minister. Replaced by a new building in 1806, which had further reconstruction in 1870, it was called Arnot Church, after their first minister. During the Revd Donald Fraser's long ministry in that church, 'On warm Sundays, when mothers could not conveniently attend the church, they came to the open church door and sat with their children on the grass, and participated in the praise and prayers.'

AN AULD LICHT.

Auld Licht, 1800s. Further splits from the Established Church followed: Burgher and Anti-Burgher, later Auld Lichts and New Lichts. Members of the Auld Licht sect were solemn and austere, their dress was staid and formal. Holding deeply religious opinions, they sang psalms every morning and evening, and J.H. Browne said, 'their faces betokened an onward gloom. They thought ... it was a sin to be happy'. Grizzel Robertson, a local member, would not comb her hair after dark 'for fear of the witches' and observed a myriad of superstitions.

Free Church, Kennoway, c.1906. In 1800 the 'Auld Lichts' built their small church in 'Laburnum Cottage' garden, where the shopping centre now stands. When their minister, Revd Adam Ross, left for Rattray, the Auld Licht congregation joined the latest section to break away from the Established Church of Scotland, due to the usual patronage issue, in the 1843 Disruption. Together they formed the Kennoway Free Church of Scotland, worshipping in the Auld Licht meeting house until the above church was built in 1848. This church closed for worship in 1985.

New Road, Kennoway, *c*.1920. The old weavers cottages, left, had been newly restored. Weavers lived in small one storey cottages, with thatched or low red pantiled roofs, which would be both their workshop and living quarters. Many weavers, often adherents of the Auld Licht sect, lived in the New Road area and the village would be quite noisy with the sound of 400 looms. In 1838 Kennoway Parish still had more than 300 weavers and 150 winders.

Weaver, 1800s. A weaver often worked as many as four looms. The weaving 'shops' were usually damp, since the dampness was beneficial to their work, but it left the weavers prone to rheumatism. Boys were employed to help and they too worked hard, standing on the damp earth with bare feet or else on their bonnets. (In 1844, children aged nine and ten were also employed in the local spinning mill, earning around 2s 6d per week.)

Politicians, c.1900. Weavers were, in the main, fine, intelligent men who took an interest in politics, holding their 'parliament' outside their cottages, like these craftsmen, to discuss the news. In the evening a weaver's shop would be the venue for discussions and for the reading of newspapers and books. Weavers worked long hours and when their candle burnt towards the end, the 'doup' was put on a small piece of wood with three small nails in it, called a 'save-all', until it was completely burnt up.

Townhead, Kennoway, c.1906. Weavers' cottages with low, thatched roofs are on the left. Many shoemakers also lived in the village, sixty-nine of them in 1836. As well as making shoes for their own customers, they produced ready-made shoes and boots for markets at Auchtermuchty, Cupar and St Andrews, to where they were transported by Stephen Pratt's cart. Latterly their main outlets were Dundee shoe shops.

Cardie Well, Kennoway Den, 1985. The waters of Cardie Well were believed to possess special healing properties in the treatment of phthisis or consumption. Cardie Well was so named because its water had been used by Italian astrologer, Jerome Cardan. He had cured Archbishop Hamilton of his asthma with spring water at Monimail Palace and while there met the Earl of Leven from nearby Melville House, who also owned Kingsdale. The villagers used water from this well on washing day, describing it as 'the everflowing spring at Carda Washinghouse'.

Washing Green, Kennoway Den, c.1907. The weekly wash was a social occasion. Early in the morning along the paths into the Den, mothers, daughters and children would make their way to work. Fires were lit to boil water for scouring the blankets and washing the sheets. On the green there were many tubs in which stood 'merry maidens with bare feet and legs tramping the clothes'. The clothes would then be spread out on the green to bleach.

Auchtermairnie Farm, Star Road, c.1960. In the nineteenth century, James Swan, tenant at Auchtermairnie Farm, was a colourful figure at harvest time in his blue dress coat with silver buttons, large black hat and yellow cashmere trousers. At harvest's end, singing and dancing went on at the farm until morning, to Sandy Wilkie's fiddle. Auchtermairnie Residential Home has been built on ground adjacent to the farm.

Aerial view, Kennoway, early 1950s. House building in the 1920s replaced old insanitary houses dating back to feudal times. Not until after the First World War was there any system of water pipes or drainage; old draw-wells or springs being the source of supply. In the 1930s, council houses were built on Leven Road, then large-scale building took place in 1948 when miners came from the West of Scotland to Fife coal fields. As well as the incoming miners, houses were also allocated to professional people, homeless people and those affected by overcrowding.

Kingsdale, c.1906. James Stark had Kingsdale built at the end of the eighteenth century, and it was acquired on his death by Miss Balfour. J.H. Browne described Kingsdale as lying snugly in the woods. A 'fine peep of the sea' could be had from the upper rooms and with its enclosed gardens it had a 'taste of delicious seclusion and refinement.' Mr Charles Cook, WS, of Edinburgh was the tenant in 1906.

Newton Hall, c.1905. In 1887 Mr G.J. Wallace, the Laird of Newton Hall, presented each of the women of Kennoway with a cup, saucer and plate suitably inscribed to commemorate the Golden Jubilee of Queen Victoria's accession to the throne. He was in turn presented with a silver cup by the villagers.

Kilmux farm buildings, 1998. Easter and Wester Kilmux were united by James Blyth Fernie, who devoted himself to agricultural improvement and the rearing of finer breeds of stock. His farm steading was the most extensive, complete and best finished in the county of Fife. He mined coal on his estate, sinking a shaft in 1835, and some 180 miners were employed by 1868. Fernie, a relative of Sir David Wilkie, tried to raise money after the artist's death to build a memorial in his native county but could not raise sufficient funds.

Kilmux House, 1998. This was built by James Blyth Fernie in 1832 and in November 1841, James, aged forty-four, married Sarah le Grand Dow, aged twenty-three, from St Ninian's, Stirling. They had three children, Andrew, Margaret and James. J.B. Fernie died in Edinburgh in 1858 and was buried in the quiet churchyard in the Causeway, Kennoway. Following a public roup at Kilmux in September 1858, Sarah and her family moved to Dollar. She died in Portobello in 1870 and was laid to rest beside her husband.

Eight
Largo and Lundin Links

Largo and Lundin Links are now almost wholly residential. Keil's Den and Dumbarnie Links are of great interest to naturalists, while on the Ladies Golf Course at Lundin Links stand the most impressive group of standing stones in Fife.

Largo. Birthplace of Alexander Selkirk.

Lower Largo, painted by David Small. In 1676, Alexander Selkirk, son of a shoemaker, was born in Lower Largo. Alexander was a rebellious youth who, tired of always being in trouble, went off to sea. As sailing master of the 'Cinque Ports', he had a major disagreement with officers and was put ashore on the deserted island of Juan Fernandez. He remained there alone for four years and four months until he was rescued by Captain Wood Rodgers, with whom he participated in some privateering before eventually arriving in London in October 1711. In Wapping he met Daniel Defoe and the writer, fascinated by his adventure story, went on to immortalize him as 'Robinson Crusoe'. In 1884 the house, shown in the inset above, replaced the original two-storey thatched cottage, and a bronze statue, designed by Stuart Burnett, Edinburgh, was unveiled by Lady Aberdeen on 11 December 1885.

Largo Bay, painted by Alexander Young. In 1860, Farnie said, 'Lundin Links lies in the recess of Largo Bay, which is said to rival the beautiful Bay of Naples...'. From June until September most houses were let to visitors, and this became one of the most popular summer resorts on the east coast. Edinburgh business men, having brought their wives, families and servants to spend a month by the seaside, would then travel daily to work in the city by train. Extra pews were brought into church aisles to accommodate summer visitors.

Lundin Links Hotel, c.1911. The Lundin Links Hotel profited from the booming tourist trade. With its red roof and gables with projecting eaves, it was built in red-pressed brick from plans prepared by Mr P.L. Henderson, Edinburgh. It had four public rooms, twenty bedrooms and the billiard room had two beautiful tables.

Leven Road, Lundin Links, c.1904. Miss Bremner was the postmistress of Lundin Mill at the shop on the left where, in the back premises, a manual telephone exchange was installed. Among the largest boarding houses in the village were Ravenswood, Elmwood, Manderlea, Lindesfarne, Victoria House and Elmbank.

Links Road, Lundin Links, early 1900s. After Sir John Gilmour succeeded to the Lundin Estate in 1884, which included the village of Lundin Mill, he had new streets, like Links Road, formed on the slopes overlooking the sand dunes and the village became increasingly known as Lundin Links, instead of Lundin Mill. Next door to the pharmacy on the corner of Links Road and Emsdorf Street was 'Park Nowe', and the villas next to that were in Park Terrace.

By the Mill Side, Lundin Links, c.1910. Lundin Mill grew up around a corn mill, to which in olden times every farmer and cottar in the district would be compelled to send their grain, a practice known as thirlage. In the mid-seventeenth century, a bridge was erected at Lundin Mill with timber which was bought in Largo from money raised by the minister and some elders. In the mid-1800s, the millers at Lundin Mill were James Ritchie (flour and barley) and William Wilson (corn and barley).

Mill Wynd, Lundin Links, c.1909. The mill, around which the hamlet grew up and from which it took its name, was probably at work on the banks of the Keil Burn more than four centuries ago. Towards the top of this picture, in what is now Largo Road, are small houses, some without roofs, which would have belonged to weavers. The principal manufacture had previously been weaving but, by 1909, few weavers would be left in the village.

Largo Harbour, 1909. Fishing in Largo had always been dependent on the appearance of herring or haddock in the bay. No mention was even made of it in the Statistical Account of 1837 for Largo Parish, but the later collapse of the linen industry rekindled interest in fishing and by 1875 there were as many as thirty-six boats, manned by eighty men and boys. The pier was the traditional mart for fishing business and exchange of news of the village. The fishermen tended their nets beside the old warehouse, later transformed into the 'snug Crusoe Inn', before taking off in their brown-sailed craft for fishing grounds in the bay.

Fairy Bridge, 1925. A footpath ran at one time from Abbotshall, Kirkcaldy to St Andrews. 'The old path was to the north of Hatton Farm, over Keil's Den by the Fairy Bridge and over the shoulder of the Law where the wood is and thence to St Andrews'.

Keil Burn and Largo Law, *c.*1950. In May 1852, when young men were leaving for the gold fields of Australia, gold mania came to Largo. Forty men assembled one Monday at the Temple of Largo before going up Largo Law to dig where gold was always thought to have been. Next day more than twice as many took part and a considerable quantity of 'gold dust' was found. The following day nearly 400 people took part! The gold rush only lasted a week – the gold dust was of no value whatever.

Serpentine, 1907. Walks were much enjoyed during the summer along the beautifully-shaded Serpentine, which connects the Temple with Upper Largo. In the nineteenth century, Tom Morgan had a shed in the Serpentine where sheep's wool was brought for the women to spin, then the men would make it into blankets. From the shed to the sea was a bleaching green, and in a hollow known as Tam's Den, at the foot of the Serpentine, owners would sit on the banks during the summer nights, keeping watch over their bleaching linen so no-one would steal it.

Nine

Transport

Transportation had for centuries been undertaken by ships from Leven and other neighbouring small harbours, while land distances had been covered by carts, carriages or coaches, all horse-drawn. The first significant change was the coming of the railway to Leven in 1854, then in the twentieth century came trams and buses. Motor cars, at first available to only the wealthier sections of society, were, by the close of the century, the most popular means of travel.

Leven Harbour c.1900. A small harbour had existed at Leven for centuries, but shifting sand in the mouth of the River Leven had always been a problem. A new dock was constructed in 1879 to cope with the expansion of the local coal industry, but the shifting sand problem and competition from the new Dock at Methil led to Leven Harbour's decline. When Mr R.G.E. Wemyss sold Methil Dock to the North British Rail Company, he included Leven Dock in the sale. The stagnant dock was subsequently considered to be a menace to the health of the community and was filled in around 1910. The steamboat in the picture is the *Sapphire*.

Leven Railway Station, 1950s. When the Leven-Thornton railway opened on 10 August 1854, shareholders and others travelled in seven carriages along the new section and were halted in some places by people waving handkerchiefs. Returning to Leven, about sixty gentlemen, including Sir Ralph Anstruther, J. Balfour of Leven Mills, and James Anderson and Robert Balfour of Durie Foundry enjoyed dinner in George Crawford's Hotel. This picture shows a small fire which occurred at the station in the 1950s.

Leven Baking Company transport, c.1890. There was a Leven Bread Society shop at 62 High Street whose manager in 1858 was James Peattie, and in 1866 was John Williamson. The name was changed in around 1873 to the Leven Co-operative Baking Company Ltd. In the 1890s Robert Annan of 18 Forth Street was secretary of the 'Leven Baking Society', perhaps another name change.

Durie Street Terminus, *c*.1906. Initially, when Mr R.G.E. Wemyss of Wemyss Castle launched his scheme to connect the towns and villages in the parishes of Wemyss and Scoonie with the burgh of Kirkcaldy, by a system of electric tramways, the line was going to terminate around Bridge Street, Leven. Following appeals from the community, however, Mr Wemyss extended the line and made the terminus in Durie Street, at the entrance to Carberry House.

Shorehead, *c*.1906. Tramcar No.9 of the Wemyss and District Tramways was one of the original tramcars, known as 'mustard boxes', and would have been in service when the tramway formally opened on 25 August 1906. Strong competition from bus services throughout the 1920s led to the demise of the tram service and the last tramcar journey on this line was made in January 1932. 'No.9' had been sold about a month earlier to Mr D. Murphy, a former track superintendent. The old tramcars were highly sought after and sold for more than £20 each.

Former Aberhill Tramcar Sheds, c.1965, now East Fife Indoor Bowling Club premises. Wemyss Coal Company powered the overhead system from an electric power station near Denbeath until 1912 when Fife Tramway Light and Power Company provided power through a transformer station at East Wemyss. At the grand opening ceremony of the tramway system, Mr Wemyss said that he hoped the tramway would be looked on as the working man's motor.

In 1925, of those who could afford a motor car, some travelled in considerable style. This lady from Largoward liked nothing better than to have day trips to Leven, Largo and Elie.

Lancia Bus, Eadie's Garage, 1920s. After the First World War, competition was not only intense between the trams and the faster buses, but also between individual bus companies. Several bus companies ferried holidaymakers around Fife during the 1920s and 1930s. They included Harris and Sons, Commercial Road, Leven; Houston and Sons and Finlay Brown's Bus Service, both of Windygates; and Milton Motor Omnibus Services, Eadie's Garage, Milton of Balgonie.

Eadie's Garage, 1920s. Dale Ross who drove the bus above is seated on the right with his fellow drivers from Eadie's Garage, Milton of Balgonie, in the 1920s. In 1936, Mr Ross was transferred to the Aberhill Depot of Alexander and Sons when they took over Eadie's Garage.

Shorehead, Leven, early 1950s. Few people owned cars but bus services were very reliable. Leven was the terminus for many long distance services – from Glasgow, Stirling and Perth – as well as local ones. It was suggested that no other town in Scotland of comparable size figured so frequently on the destination board of buses. Bus conductresses collected fares at that time; 'one-person' operated buses were for the future.

In 1959, at a time when families were aspiring to own their first motor car, T. MacDonald & Sons were a well-known local firm to whom they would go. In the days before Value Added Tax, purchase tax had to be added to the quoted price, including the tuppence!

116

Ten

Youth

When Mitchell Street school was built, the curriculum was mainly concerned with the teaching of the three R's - reading, 'riting and 'rithmetic. In the 1960s, comprehensive education was introduced, the 11-plus and junior secondary schools were abolished, and a new high school, Kirkland, was built at Crossroads. Many young people belonged to youth organizations such as Girls' Guildry (now Girls' Brigade), Boys' Brigade, Girl Guides and Boy Scouts.

Leven Public School, Mitchell Street, 1881. The school had both Elementary and Higher Grade Departments. In March 1900 when Mr Calder, of cinematograph fame, offered pupils a free exhibition in the Town Hall, there were no absentees! All minor ailments as well as such drawbacks as 'leaky boots and torn jackets' were forgotten. They marched in perfect order from the playground to the Town Hall, where, including adults, around 1,200 people were accommodated in a hall meant to hold 800. The numbers on the school roll in the early 1900s were over 1,250 in the Elementary Department and seventy in the Higher Grade.

Parkhill School, c.1910. To relieve the overcrowding in the Mitchell Street School – many children were being taught in local halls – Parkhill Public School was built and opened in 1910, accommodating 480 children. Parkhill School, now a listed building, is still in use as a primary school, but the Mitchell Street School, which latterly became a branch of Glenrothes and Buckhaven College of Technology, was demolished in around 1996 and the Lidl supermarket was built on the site.

These two Leven schoolgirls were photographed in their Sunday best in the Talbot Studio, Station Road, c.1912. The Misses Charlotte Bramwell and Annie Ferguson had taken over the studio which had been established by Adam Diston.

Viewforth Nursery, 1993. The original purpose of this building, opposite the main Mitchell Street School, was to house the Woodwork and Cookery Departments of the school. It was refurbished in 1976 and converted for use as a nursery for pre-school children.

Viewforth Nursery, session 1976/77. Miss Sheena McCallum was Headmistress of Viewforth Nursery School when it opened in 1976, and staff members were Mrs Edith Steele, Mrs Alex Crawford and Mrs Anne Robertson. From left, Julie Cameron, Stephen Moore, Mrs Steele, Heather Caldwell, Alan Turnbull, Mrs Crawford, Stephen Nelson, -?-, Miss McCallum, -?-, -?-, Mrs Robertson, Ian Belford, Adele Baxter, Paul ?.

Braehead Secondary School, 1957. Originally known as Madras School, this was Buckhaven High School from 1933 until 1957, when it became Braehead Secondary, a progressive school under headmaster, R.F. MacKenzie. Mountaineer and author, Hamish Brown, a teacher there, took parties of boys on outward bound trips in the Highlands. They developed a great interest in wildlife and made a lasting impression on Gavin Maxwell, the author, at his home in Sandaig. The radical ideals of Braehead influenced Maxwell, who became a convinced opponent of the exam-orientated education system. He encouraged sixteen year-old Richard Branson, who had just won the Gavin Maxwell Prize, to abandon his studies at top school, Stowe, and begin his entrepreneurial career immediately.

Buckhaven High School, 1957. Buckhaven High School had been severely overcrowded in the old building in Buckhaven and had been using six buildings scattered on both sides of College Street, including a church hall. This new building, surrounded by acres of playing fields, opened in 1957. The buses of W. Alexander & Sons awaited the afternoon rush.

Official Opening, Assembly Hall, Buckhaven High School, October 1957. Teachers include Mr Marshall, Mr Currie, Mr Goodwin, Miss N. Anderson, Miss Rennie, Mr Pearson, Mr Gowans, Mr Sam Clarke, Mr Ruthven, Mr MacDonald, Mr Tom Fraser and Mr McPhee.

W.S. Byres, *c*.1960. Mr Byres was Rector of Buckhaven High School for over eighteen years. During this period he encountered wartime difficulties followed by post-war shortages of staff and accommodation. In January 1962, on his retirement, he quipped that, during the war, when he had allowed pupils to have a half-day holiday following the dropping of a bomb near Windygates, some wit had said it would take another bomb before they would get another. However, he reminded everyone that this was not so as he sent pupils home following a heating failure at the new school!

'Prometheus Bound', 1957. This sculpture, which stood at the entrance to the new high school, was created by Andrew G.P. Buchan, teacher of Art at Kirkcaldy High School, who was a regular exhibitor at the Royal Scottish Academy. He died in 1960, aged thirty-six. Unfortunately, no trace remains today of 'Prometheus', as it was vandalized many years ago.

John Wallace, 1962. He won the Individual Cup for Music at Buckhaven High School in 1962, and read Music at King's College, Cambridge. He joined the London Symphony Orchestra before becoming Principal Trumpet Player of the Philharmonic Orchestra, where he remained for twenty years. A world-class trumpet soloist, he has created a new brass ensemble, the Wallace Collection. Currently Principal Trumpet of the London Sinfonietta, he was awarded the OBE in 1995 in recognition of his services to music.

First Year Football Team, 1957. Among the boys with Mr Robb were: ? Connolly, A. Barnett, J. Caldwell, J. Falls, I. Levack, E. McMurdo, J. Goldie and J. Black.

Parkhill Primary School, 1981. P7 boys won the Primary Schools Area Championship for golf while the girls won the Pamela Brown Cup for netball and were area league winners. Back, from left, Mrs Margaret Moyes (in charge of golf), Graham Herd, Stewart Kirkwood, Barry Deas, Barry Hastie, Gavin Welsh, Neil McAndrew and Mrs Christina Herd, netball organiser. Front row, Sheena Martin, Judith Keenlyside, Karen Mitchell, Angela Caldwell, Tracy Reid, Kerry Lipton and Michelle Pirret.

Rover Scout Moot, Inchcolm 1960. Boys from local Boy Scout companies moved on to this Rover Scout troupe at East Wemyss. Led by John Carstairs, they used a Scout hut in the Den below East Wemyss Primary School. From left, J. Greenhorn, C. Wilson, J. Caldwell, A. McColl, -?-, Mr J. Carstairs, D. Hopper, and District Commissioner, Mr Reid.

2nd Leven Guides, March 1984. Queen's Guide Certificates were awarded to six girls of 2nd Leven Guide Company in the Bain Hall by Chief Constable, William M. Moodie. From left, Melanie Jappy, Mrs M. Cunningham, Assistant Guider, Jane Brodie, Angela Caldwell, Mr Moodie, Gillian Moore, Elaine Connell, Mrs M. Chisholm, Guider, and Shiona Hughes. This was the last presentation to be made in Leven of Queen's Guide Certificates before these were replaced by the Baden-Powell Award.

Eleven
Events

These images begin with events from the early twentieth century and end with the crowning of the first Leven Rose Queen of the new millennium.

By the Swan Pond, Leven, 6 June 1912. Mr Wright and his station staff had to cope with five special trains carrying 500 people, while Wemyss tramcars brought a record 12,000 people to the 42nd Gala of Fife and Kinross Miner's Association at Leven. Led by bands, they made their way from the station to the Town Hall, where they were welcomed by Provost Balfour, Bailie Lawrence and Councillor Mackie. Following their meeting, some went to the bowling green, some to the Links, and some to Bayview for sports, while others went to the Drill Hall for the ambulance competition. Fifteen miners' leaders were entertained by Provost Balfour at Carberry House. At Linnwood Hall, where Charles Carlow provided dinner for around forty veteran miners of East and West Fife, a recital was given on the organ by Mr John Stalker of St John's UF Church, and later in the day Kelty Prize Band played in the grounds.

Leven Town Hall, 22 June 1908. Prior to his intended visit to South Africa, General William Booth, aged seventy-nine, founder of the Salvation Army, made a farewell tour of Central Scotland. Travelling in his distinctive white motor car, he arrived in Leven to be greeted by the Town Council delegation, headed by Provost Balfour, at the Town Hall. Flags and streamers flew from the Hall as well as many private buildings and a great enthusiastic crowd gathered. The General was presented to Provost Balfour and Councillors Aitken, Barron, Mackie and Lawrence. General Booth was later entertained at Linnwood Hall, home of Charles Carlow. When the white motor and accompanying cars left at 6 o'clock the General stood up in the 'machine' and waved as it swept past the crowds lining the street nearly the whole way to Leven Bridge.

General Booth, with his long flowing beard, leaving the Leven Town Hall.

Parkhill School, June 1977. Parkhill, Mountfleurie and St Agatha Schools participated in a Silver Jubilee Sports Festival at George V Park. Parkhill Primary School won the championship and presentations took place at Parkhill School, with the school's Primary 7 pupils. Mr Tommy Laing, Park Superintendent, left, organized the event and Mr Jim Drysdale, East Fife Director, donated the trophy. Heather Caldwell was the Jubilee Princess.

June 2000. Eleven year old Lindsay Peter, of Parkhill Primary School, was the Millennium Rose Queen. On Saturday 10 June 2000, at Carberry House, she was crowned by Betty Henderson, who was the first ever Rose Queen in 1938.

LEVEN

HERALDIC SERIES.

Acknowledgements

Photographic Sources:
James Donaldson & Sons Ltd; East Fife Mail; Fife Leader; George Harvey; Save the Wemyss Ancient Caves Society; Scottish Fisheries Museum Trust Ltd, Anstruther; Miss Ella Smith; Tom Smith and Harry Fraser; White Postcards; Valentine Postcards: Copyright St Andrew's University Library.

Thanks to the above for permission to use these photographs and to Jerzy T. Morkis, Group Editor, Fife Free Press Group for permission to use the Leven Mail and East Fife Mail to check particular dates and for general research. Thanks also to Elaine Grey, Writer's Museum; Miss Jean Donaldson and Deborah Palmer, Donaldson & Sons; Julia Stephen, Mining Museum; Miss McGowan, Scottish Fisheries Museum, Anstruther.

Special thanks also to Mrs Anne Watters for her encouragement and to Jack and Angela for their support. Finally to Heather for her support and for the many postcards she has gifted to me over the years, making this project possible.